THE PENGUIN POETS

# LONDON

.

## *In Verse*

Christopher Logue is a young seventy-nine. He has done a little writing, and almost no acting. The famous cineast, Mr Patrick Marnham, has described him as 'the man in the wrong film'. In accordance with Government policy, Christopher Logue is half-employed (on a fortnightly basis) by Lord Gnome.

'What a place to plunder!'

Field Marshal Gebhard Leberecht von Blücher

Said when viewing London from the dome of St Paul's Cathedral, and after attending a Peace Banquet in Oxford, in 1814.

# LONDON

•

# *In Verse*

•

edited, with notes, and with
illustrations chosen by

# CHRISTOPHER LOGUE

That certain night, the night we met
There was magic abroad in the air,
There were angels dining at the Ritz
And a nightingale sang in Berkeley Square.

Eric Maschwitz

Penguin Books

Penguin Books Ltd, Harmondsworth, Middlesex, England
Penguin Books, 40 West 23rd Street, New York, New York 10010, U.S.A.
Penguin Books Australia Ltd, Ringwood, Victoria, Australia
Penguin Books Canada Ltd, 2801 John Street, Markham, Ontario, Canada L3R 1B4
Penguin Books (N.Z.) Ltd, 182–190 Wairau Road, Auckland 10, New Zealand

First published in Great Britain by Martin Secker & Warburg Ltd 1982
Published in Penguin Books 1984

Regions in Verse series. General Editor: Emma Tennant

Made and printed in Great Britain by
Richard Clay (The Chaucer Press) Ltd, Bungay, Suffolk
Set in Monophoto Ehrhardt

To my friends
Kenny and Alice Carter
their sons
Douglas and Christopher
and
Valerie Sullivan
her husband and her children

And to my neighbours
Terry and Lyn Mitchell
Trudy Weaver
Queenie Housego and her daughter, Jane,
Rod Buck
Manley Black
Harry Major and his son, Robert,
Patrick and Margaret Spencer and their son, Joe,
Reg and Bridget Vaughan and their daughter, Juliet,
Monica Anthony
David Chance
Betty Mylius
Michael and Rose Cohen
Anabel Weaver
Harry Lander
Adrian and Annie Nolan
Peter Stork
Elaine Roskilly

*Samuel Johnson on London in 1738*

Here Malice, Rapine, Accident, conspire,
And now a Rabble rages, now a Fire;
Their Ambush here relentless Ruffians lay,
And here the fell Attorney prowls for Prey.

*and in 1777*

Why, Sir, you find no man, at all intellectual,
who is willing to leave London. No, Sir, when a
man is tired of London, he is tired of life; for
there is in London all that life can afford.

# CONTENTS

This is the most famous panegyric to London. William Dunbar came to London in 1501 as a member of an embassy sent to arrange the marriage of Scotland's King, James IV, to Margaret Tudor, the eldest daughter of Henry VII. Some say that Dunbar recited his poem at a banquet given by the Lord Mayor.

London, thou art of townes A *per se*.
   Soveraign of cities, semeliest in sight,
Of high renoun, riches, and royaltie;
   Of lordis, barons, and many goodly knyght;
   Of most delectable lusty ladies bright;
Of famous prelatis in habitis clericall;
   Of merchauntis full of substaunce and myght:
London, thou art the flour of Cities all.

Gladdith anon, thou lusty Troy Novaunt,
   Citie that some tyme cleped was New Troy,
In all the erth, imperiall as thou stant,
   Pryncesse of townes, of pleasure, and of joy,
   A richer restith under no Christen roy;
For manly power, with craftis naturall,
   Fourmeth none fairer sith the flode of Noy:
London, thou art the flour of Cities all.

Gemme of all joy, jasper of jocunditie,
   Most myghty carbuncle of vertue and valour;
Strong Troy in vigour and in strenuitie;
   Of royall cities rose and geraflour;
   Empresse of townes, exalt in honour;
In beawtie beryng the crone imperiall;
   Swete paradise precelling in pleasure:
London, thou art the flour of Cities all.

Above all ryvers thy Ryver hath renowne,
   Whose beryall stremys, pleasaunt and preclare,
Under thy lusty wallys renneth down,

Where many a swanne doth swymme with wyngis fare;
Where many a barge doth saile, and row with are,
Where many a ship doth rest with toppe-royall.
   O! towne of townes, patrone and not-compare:
London, thou art the flour of Cities all.

Upon thy lusty Brigge of pylers white
   Been merchauntis full royall to behold;
Upon thy sretis goth many a semely knyght
   In velvet gownes and cheynes of fyne gold.
   By Julyus Cesar thy Tour founded of old
May be the hous of Mars victoryall,
   Whos artillary with tonge may not be told:
London, thou art the flour of Cities all.

Strong by thy wallis that about the standis;
   Wise by the people that within the dwellis;
Fresh is thy ryver with his lusty strandis;
   Blith be thy chirches, wele sownyng be thy bellis;
   Riche be thy merchauntis in substaunce that excellis;
Fair be thy wives, right lovesom, white and small;
Clere be thy virgyns, lusty under kellis:
London, thou art the flour of Cities all.

Thy famous Maire, by pryncely governaunce,
   With swerd of justice the rulith prudently.
No Lord of Parys, Venyce, or Floraunce
   In dignytie or honoure goeth to hym nye.
   He is exampler, loode-ster, and guye;
Principall patrone and roose orygynalle,
   Above all Maires as maister moost worthy:
London, thou art the flour of Cities all.

### WILLIAM DUNBAR
### [1465?–1530?]

Mentioned: *strenuitie*, constraint; *geraflour*, pink, wallflower, or stock; *preclare*, dazzling, bright; *kellis*, headdresses; *guye*, guide.

A typical invoice for a banquet such as Dunbar attended would have been:

|  | s. | d. |
|---|---|---|
| Great Beeves, from the shambles, twenty-four, each | 26 | 8 |
| One carcass of an Ox — — — | 24 | 0 |
| Fat Muttons, one hundred, each — — | 2 | 10 |
| Great Veals, fifty-one, each — — | 4 | 8 |
| Porks, thirty-four, each — — — | 3 | 8 |
| Pigs, ninety-one, each — — — | 0 | 6 |
| Capons of Greece (of one Poulterer, for they had three) ten dozen, each Capon — — | 1 | 8 |
| Capons of Kent, nine dozen and six, ditto — | 1 | 0 |
| Capons, coarse, nineteen dozen, ditto — | 0 | 6 |
| Cocks of grose [Grouse?] seven dozen and nine, each cock — — — — | 0 | 8 |
| Cocks, coarse, fourteen dozen and eight, ditto | 0 | 3 |
| Pullets, the best, each — — — | 0 | 2½ |
| Other Pullets, each — — — | 0 | 2 |
| Pidgeons, thirty-seven dozen, per dozen — | 0 | 10 |
| Swans, twenty-four dozen — — — |  |  |
| Larks, 30 dozen, per dozen — — | 0 | 5 |

## *The Lover to the Thames of London to Favour His Lady Passing Thereon*

Thou stately stream that with the swelling tide
'Gainst London walls incessantly dost beat,
Thou Thames, I say, where barge and boat doth ride,
And snow-white swans do fish for needful meat:

When so my love, of force or pleasure, shall
Flit on thy flood as custom is to do,
Seek not with dread her courage to appal,
But calm thy tide, and smoothly let it go,
As she may joy, arrived to siker shore,
To pass the pleasant stream she did before.

To welter up and surge in wrathful wise,
As did the flood where Hell drenchëd was,
Would but procure defame of thee to rise:
Wherefore let all such ruthless rigour pass,
So wish I that thou may'st with bending side
Have power for aye in wonted gulf to glide.

GEORGE TURBERVILLE
[1540?–1610?]

In South America there are more statues of Lord Byron than of any other British poet. Wanting, in 1981, to honour a locally born poet called José Olmedo, but without the means to commission an original monument, the people of Guayaquil, Ecuador, bought a second-hand statue of Byron and put Olmedo's name on it.

## From *Don Juan*, Cantos 10, 11 and 13

> . . . Juan now was borne,
> Just as the day began to wane and darken,
>     O'er the high hill which looks with pride or scorn
> Towards the great city. Ye who have a spark in
>     Your veins of Cockney spirit smile or mourn,
> According as you take things well or ill.
> Bold Britons, we are now on Shooter's Hill.
>
> The sun went down, the smoke rose up, as from
>     A half-unquenched volcano, o'er a space
> Which well beseemed the 'devil's drawing room',
>     As some have qualified that wondrous place.
> But Juan felt, though not approaching home,
>     As one who, though he were not of the race,
> Revered the soil, of those true sons the mother,
> Who butchered half the earth and bullied t'other.
>
> A mighty mass of brick and smoke and shipping,
>     Dirty and dusky, but as wide as eye
> Could reach, with here and there a sail just skipping
>     In sight, then lost amidst the forestry
> Of masts, a wilderness of steeples peeping
>     On tiptoe through their sea coal canopy,
> A huge, dun cupola, like a foolscap crown
> On a fool's head – and there is London town!

. . . Hail, Thamis, hail! Upon thy verge it is
That Juan's chariot, rolling like a drum
 In thunder, holds the way it can't well miss,
Through Kennington and all the other 'tons',
Which makes us wish ourselves in town at once;

Through groves, so called as being void of trees
 (Like *lucus* from no light); through prospects named
Mount Pleasant, as containing nought to please
 Nor much to climb; through little boxes framed
Of bricks, to let the dust in at your ease,
 With 'To be let' upon their doors proclaimed;
Through 'Rows' most modestly called 'Paradise',
Which Eve might quit without much sacrifice;

Through coaches, drays, choked turnpikes, and a whirl
 Of wheels, and roar of voices and confusion.
Here taverns wooing to a pint of 'purl';
 There mails fast flying off like a delusion;
There barber's blocks with periwigs in curl
 In windows; here the lamplighter's infusion
Slowly distilled into the glimmering glass
(For in those days we had not got to gas).

Through this and much and more is the approach
 Of travellers to mighty Babylon.
Whether they come by horse or chaise or coach,
 With slight exceptions, all the ways seem one.
I could say more, but do not choose to encroach
 Upon the guidebook's privilege. The sun
Had set some time, and night was on the ridge
Of twilight as the party crossed the bridge.

That's rather fine, the gentle sound of Thamis,
 Who vindicates a moment too his stream,
Though hardly heard through multifarious 'damme's'.
 The lamps of Westminster's more regular gleam,

The breadth of pavement, and yon shrine where Fame is
    A spectral resident, whose pallid beam
In shape of moonshine hovers o'er the pile,
Make this a sacred part of Albion's isle.

The Druid's groves are gone – so much the better.
    Stonehenge is not, but what the devil is it?
But Bedlam still exists with its sage fetter,
    That madmen may not bite you on a visit.
The Bench too seats or suits full many a debtor.
    The Mansion House too (though some people quiz it)
To me appears a stiff yet grand erection.
But then the Abbey's worth the whole collection.

Over the stones still rattling up Pall Mall
    Through crowds and carriages, but waxing thinner
As thundered knockers broke the long-sealed spell
    Of doors 'gainst duns, and to an early dinner
Admitted a small party as night fell,
    Don Juan, our young diplomatic sinner,
Pursued his path and drove past some hotels,
St James's Palace and St James's hells.

They reached the hotel. Forth streamed from the front door
    A tide of well-clad waiters, and around
The mob stood and as usual several score
    Of those pedestrian Paphians, who abound
In decent London when the daylight's o'er.
    Commodious but immoral, they are found
Useful, like Malthus, in promoting marriage.
But Juan now is stepping from his carriage

Into one of the sweetest of hotels,
    Especially for foreigners and mostly
For those whom favour or whom fortune swells
    And cannot find a bill's small items costly.

There many an envoy either dwelt or dwells
   (The den of many a diplomatic lost lie),
Until to some conspicuous square they pass
And blazon o'er the door their names in brass.

'Tis true I might have chosen Piccadilly,
   A place where peccadilloes are unknown,
But I have motives, whether wise or silly,
   For letting that pure sanctuary alone.
Therefore I name not square, street, place, until I
   Find one where nothing naughty can be shown,
A vestal shrine of innocence of heart.
Such are – but I have lost the London chart.

## LORD BYRON
## [1788–1824]

Mentioned: *yon shrine where Fame is*, Poets' Corner in Westminster Abbey; *Bedlam*, Bethlehem Hospital for lunatics (demolished); *The Bench*, the Court of Common Pleas; *Mansion House*, the Official Residence of the Lord Mayor of London; *Abbey*, Westminster Abbey; *Stonehenge*, a collection of large stones on Salisbury Plain whose disposition excites the credulous; *St James's Palace*, the royal residence in London until it burned down in 1809; *St James's hells*, fashionable casinos; *Paphians*, prostitutes and their clients; *Malthus*, T. R. Malthus (1766–1834), a mad curate who thought that the rich should be encouraged to breed.

## The Aldermen of London

In 1800 this pompous body gave a banquet at the Vintners' Hall: 'A handsome building; its gates have stone piers sculptured with grapes and vine leaves; by one of its windows is a painting of a sundial with a flea upon it.' At the banquet this verse was recited:

Water I loathe,
Said Alderman Trothe;
Port I absorb,
Said Alderman Corb;
This claret's quite sour,
Said Alderman Flower;
Port against claret,
Said Alderman Garrett;
I like either if good,
Said Alderman Wood;
Sham-pag-nay, a spur 'tis,
Said Alderman Curtis;
Champaigne, not Shampagnay,
Said Alderman Magnay;
'Tis true what he saith man,
Said Alderman Waithman;
This port's of a flat kin,
Said Alderman Atkin;
Its crust is quite thin,
Said Alderman Glyn;
Its heat is prodigious,
Said Alderman Bridges;
Some sherry forthwith,
Said Alderman Smith;

I can't get it down,
Said Alderman Brown;
Its as dead as a herring,
Said Alderman Perring;
Its as cold as a church,
Said Alderman Birch;
If so, then pray egg it,
Said Alderman Heygate;
No mixture – wine solely,
Said Alderman Scholey;
Some liqueurs from that box,
Said Alderman Cox;
Ah! some nice usquebaugh,
Said Alderman Shaw;
'Tis not in the dinner bills,
Said Alderman Venables;
Now if this way some Nantz lay,
Said Alderman Ansley;
Ah! Nantz is life's bunter,
Said Alderman Hunter;
Then with Nantz keep our romps on,
Said Alderman Thompson.

[*c.* 1800]

Mentioned: *usquebaugh*, whisky; *Nantz*, brandy from Nantes on the Loire, France.

# A Fashionable Lady at Church

Tom D'Urfey (1653–1723), thought to have been the author of this piece, was his time's most successful writer of song lyrics. Queen Anne (1665–1714) gave him fifty guineas for writing the words of a song about the Electress Sophia – who was next in line for the throne – that began: 'The crown's far too weighty, for shoulders of eighty'. D'Urfey's *Wit and Mirth, or Pills to Purge Melancholy* (1720) is one of the best collections of British songs. He died poor.

## *St James's Prayers*

Last Sunday at St James's prayers,
    The prince and princess by,
I, drest in all my whale-bone airs,
    Sat in a closet nigh.
I bow'd my knees, I held my book,
    Read all the answers o'er;
But was perverted by a look,
    Which pierced me from the door.
High thoughts of Heaven I came to use,
    With the devoutest care,
Which gay young Strephon made me lose,
    And all the raptures there.
He stood to hand me to my chair,
    And bow'd with courtly grace;
But whisper'd love into my ear,
    Too warm for that grave place.
'Love, love,' said he, 'by all adored,
    My tender heart has won.'
But I grew peevish at the word,
    And bade he would be gone.
He went quite out of sight, while I
    A kinder answer meant;
Nor did I for my sins that day
    By half so much repent.

[c. 1720]

## Life–Guardsman

Joy of the Milliner, Envy of the Line,
Star of the Parks, jack-booted, sworded, helmed,
He sits between his holsters, solid of spine;
Nor, as it seems, though Westminster were whelmed,
With the great globe, in earthquake and eclipse,
Would he and his charger cease from mounting guard,
This Private in the Blues, nor would his lips
Move, though his gorge with throttled oaths were charred!
He wears his inches weightily, as he wears
His old-world armours; and with his port and pride,
His sturdy graces and enormous airs,
He towers in speech his Colonel countrified,
    A triumph, waxing statelier year by year,
    Of British blood, and bone, and beef, and beer.

W. E. HENLEY
[1849–1903]

*Horse Guards' Parade, East Front*

# Miss Knightsbridge

I'm eighteen actually, although
Most people take me for *much* more;
I'm *not* a debutante, you know.
I think it's *such* a bore to go
To parties until three or four.
My father was an aide-de-camp.
We've got an aubergine front door.
I'm *frightfully* keen on Terence Stamp.

I *wish* I had a bigger bust,
Though Mummy says it's frightfully smart
And any more would beckon lust.
She says I absolutely *must*
Stop trying to be keen on art
And dressing like a King's Road tramp.
I simply don't know where to start.
I'm *frightfully* keen on Terence Stamp.

I'm starting on a course quite soon,
It's sort of cookery and flowers.
My latest colour's deep maroon.
And sometimes in the afternoon
I simply lie for hours and hours
Beneath dear Mummy's sun-ray lamp
And contemplate the Carlton Towers.
I'm *frightfully* keen on Terence Stamp.

CANDIDA LYCETT GREEN
[b. 1942]

# The Lament of the Banana Man

Gal, I'm tellin' you, I'm tired fo' true
Tired of Englan', tired o' you.
But I can't go back to Jamaica now . . .

I'm here in Englan', I'm drawin' pay,
I go to de underground every day –
Eight hours is all, half-hour fo' lunch,
M' uniform's free, an' m' ticket punch –
Punchin' tickets not hard to do,
When I'm tired o' punchin', I let dem through.

I get a paid holiday once a year.
Ol' age an' sickness can't touch me here.
I have a room of m'own, an' a iron bed,
Dunlopillo under m' head,
A Morphy-Richards to warm de air,
A formica table, an easy chair.
I have summer clothes, an' winter clothes,
An' paper kerchiefs to blow m' nose.

My yoke is easy, my burden is light,
I know a place I can go to, any night.
Dis place Englan'! I'm not complainin',
If it col', it col', if it rainin', it rainin'.
I don't min' if it's mostly night,
Dere's always inside, or de sodium light.
I don't min' white people starin' at me,
Dey don' want me here? Don't is deir country?
You won' catch me bawlin' any homesick tears,
If I don' see Jamaica for a t'ousan' years!

. . . Gal, I'm tellin' you, I'm tired fo' true,
Tired of Englan', tired o' you,
I can't go back to Jamaica now –
But I'd want to die there, anyhow.

EVAN JONES

# LAWYERS

The Inner and Middle Temples have always housed London's lawyers. Pegasus, the winged horse, is the insignia of the Middle, and the Holy Lamb of the Inner Temple. These rhymes date from the eighteenth century

As by the Templars' holds you go,
　　The Horse and Lamb display'd,
In emblematic figures shew
　　The merits of their trade.

That clients may infer from thence
　　How just is their profession,
The Lamb sets forth their Innocence,
　　The Horse their Expedition.

Oh happy Britons! Happy Isle!
　　Let foreign Nations say,
Where you get Justice without guile,
　　And Law without delay!

*

Deluded men, these holds forego,
　　Nor trust such cunning elves;
These artful emblems tend to shew
　　Their Clients, not Themselves.

'Tis all a trick; these are all shams
　　By which they mean to cheat you;
But have a care, for you're the Lambs,
　　And they the Wolves that eat you.

Nor let the thoughts of 'no delay,'
　　To these their Courts misguide you;
'Tis you're the shewy Horse, and they
　　The Jockies that will ride you.

## SAUSAGE SELLERS

'The wretched vendors of sausages, who cared not what they made them of, such as those about forty years back [1800] who fried them in cellars in St Giles's, and under gateways in Drury Lane, Field Lane, commonly called 'Food and Raiment Alley or Thieving Lane, alias Sheep's Head Alley', with all its courts and ramifications of Black Boy Alley, Saffron Hill, Bleeding Heart Yard, and Cow Cross, were continually persecuting their unfortunate neighbours, to whom they were as offensive as the melters of tallow, bone burners, soap boilers, or cat-gut cleaners. This 'Food and Raiment Alley', so named from the cook and old clothes shops, was in former days so dangerous to go through, that it was scarcely possible for a person to possess his watch or his handkerchief by the time he had passed this ordeal of infamy; and it is a fact, that a man after losing his pocket-handkerchief, might, on his immediate return through the Lane, see it exposed for sale, and purchase it at half the price it originally cost him, of the mother of the young gentleman who had so dextrously deprived him of it. They cry:'

> Come, Mistress, buy this dainty pound.
> About a chicken roast them round.

## SIMPLERS

'The Simpler commences her selections from the ditches and swampy grounds at that early period of the day, and, after she has filled a large pack for her back, trudges for fifteen miles to the London markets. Simplers are much attached to brass rings, which they display in great profusion upon almost every finger: their faces and arms are sunburnt and freckled, and they live to a great age, notwithstanding their constant wet and heavy burthens, which are always carried on the loins. They cry:'

Here's fine rosemary, sage, and thyme!
Come buy my ground ivy.
Here's fetherfew, gilliflowers, and rue,
Come buy my knotted marjorum, ho!
Come buy my mint, my fine green mint,
Here's fine lavender for your clothes,
Here's parsley and winter-savory,
And hearts-ease, which all do choose.
Here's balm and hissop, and cinquefoil,
All fine herbs, it is well known.
   Let none despise the merry merry Cries
   Of famous London Town!

Here's pennyroyal and marigolds!
Come buy my nettle-tops.
Here's water-cresses and scurvy-grass!
Come buy my sage of virtue ho!
Come buy my wormwood and mugwort,
Here's all fine herbs of every sort.
Here's southernwood that's very good,
Dandelion and houseleek.
Here's dragon's tongue and wood sorrel,
With bear's foot and horehound.
   Let none despise the merry merry Cries
   Of famous London Town!

JOHN THOMAS SMITH,
*The Cries of London* [1839]

## Miss Hamilton in London

It would not be true to say she was doing nothing:
She visited several bookshops, spent an hour
In the Victoria and Albert Museum (Indian section),
And walked carefully through the streets of Kensington
Carrying five mushrooms in a paper bag,
A tin of black pepper, a literary magazine,
And enough money to pay the rent for two weeks.
The sky was cloudy, leaves lay on the pavements.

Nor did she lack human contacts: she spoke
To three shop-assistants and a newsvendor,
And returned the 'Goodnight' of a museum attendant.
Arriving home, she wrote a letter to someone
In Canada, as it might be, or in New Zealand,
Listening to the news as she cooked her meal,
And conversed for five minutes with the landlady.
The air was damp with the mist of late autumn.

A full day, and not unrewarding.
Night fell at the usual seasonal hour.
She drew the curtains, switched on the electric fire,
Washed her hair and read until it was dry,
Then went to bed; where, for the hours of darkness,
She lay pierced by thirty black spears
And felt her limbs numb, her eyes burning,
And dark rust carried along her blood.

FLEUR ADCOCK
[b. 1934]

## Caleb Quotem, Clerk and
## Sexton to the Parish of Moorfields

I'm parish clerk and sexton here;
My name is Caleb Quotem:
I'm painter, glazier, auctioneer;
In short, I am *factotum*.
I make a watch – I mend the pumps;
For plumber's work my nack is:
I physic sell – I cure the mumps;
I tombstones cut – I cut the rumps
Of little school boy Jackies.
Geography is my delight;
Ballads – epitaphs I write;
Almanacks I can indite;
Graves I dig compact and tight.
At dusk, by the fire, like a good jolly cook,
When my day's work is done and all over,
I tipple, I smoke, and I wind up the clock,
With my sweet Mrs Quotem in clover.

[c. 1750]

# The Ruined Maid

'O 'Melia, my dear, this does everything crown!
Who could have supposed I should meet you in Town?
And whence such fair garments, such prosperi-ty?' –
'O didn't you know I'd been ruined?' said she.

– 'You left us in tatters, without shoes or socks,
Tired of digging potatoes, and spudding up docks;
And now you've gay bracelets and bright feathers three!' –
'Yes: that's how we dress when we're ruined,' said she.

– 'At home in the barton you said "thee" and "thou",
And "thik oon", and "theäs oon", and "t'other"; but now
Your talking quite fits 'ee for high compa-ny!' –
'Some polish is gained with one's ruin,' said she.

– 'Your hands were like paws then, your face blue and bleak
But now I'm bewitched by your delicate cheek,
And your little gloves fit as on any la-dy!' –
'We never do work when we're ruined,' said she.

– 'You used to call home-life a hag-ridden dream,
And you'd sigh, and you'd sock; but at present you seem
To know not of megrims or melancho-ly!' –
'True. One's pretty lively when ruined,' said she.

– 'I wish I had feathers, a fine sweeping gown,
And a delicate face, and could strut about Town!' –
'My dear – a raw country girl, such as you be,
Cannot quite expect that. You ain't ruined,' said she.

THOMAS HARDY
[1840–1928]

# THE CLUBMAN

Captain Morris was a fine songwriter and a fair singer. He served in the
17th Foot and the 2nd Life Guards and may well have been the author of
*The Great Plenipotentiary*, an obscene song composed to celebrate
Admiral Edward Pellew's attack on Algiers in 1816. The first stanza goes:

> The Dey of Algiers, when afraid for his ears,
>     A messenger sent to our Court, Sirs;
> As he knew in our State that the women have weight,
>     He chose one well-hung for good sport, Sirs;
> So he searched his Divan and promoted a man
>     Whose danglers were heavy and hairy,
> And who lately came o'er, from the Barbary Shore,
>     As the Great Plenipotentiary. . .

When he was old and poor, Captain Morris was given a pension of £200
a year by the Prince of Wales.

## *The Town and the Country*

> In London I never know what I'd be at,
> Enraptured with this, and enchanted with that;
> I'm wild with the sweets of Variety's plan,
> And Life seems a blessing too happy for man.
>
> But the Country, God help me! sets all matters right,
> So calm and composing from morning to night;
> Oh! it settles the spirits when nothing is seen
> But an ass on a common, a goose on a green.
>
> In town we've no use for the skies overhead,
> For when the sun rises then we go to bed;

And as to that old-fashioned virgin the moon,
She shines out of season, like satin in June.

In the country what bliss, when it rains in the fields,
To live on the transports that shuttlecock yields;
Or go crawling from window to window, to see
A pig on a dunghill, or crow on a tree.

In London, if folks ill together are put,
A *bore* may be dropp'd, and a *quiz* may be cut:
We change without end; and if lazy or ill,
All wants are at hand, and all wishes at will.

In the country you're nail'd, like a pale in the park,
To some *stick* of a neighbour that's cramm'd in the ark;
And 'tis odds, if you're hurt, or in fits tumble down,
You reach death ere the doctor can reach you from town.

In London how easy we visit and meet,
Gay pleasure's the theme, and sweet smiles are our treat;
Our morning's a round of good humour'd delight,
And we rattle, in comfort, to pleasure at night.

In the country, how sprightly! our visits we make
Through ten miles of mud, for Formality's sake;
With the coachman in drink, and the moon in a fog,
And no thought in your head but a ditch or a bog.

But 'tis in the country alone we can find
That happy resource, that relief to the mind,
When, drove to despair, our last effort we make,
And drag the old fish-pond, for Novelty's sake:

Indeed I must own, 'tis a pleasure complete
To see ladies well draggled and wet in their feet;
But what is all that to the transport we feel
When we capture, in triumph, two toads and an eel?

Your magpies and stock-doves may flirt among trees,
And chatter their transports in groves, if they please;
But a house is much more to my taste than a tree,
And for groves, oh! a good grove of chimneys for me.

In the country, if Cupid should find a man out,
The poor tortured victim mopes hopeless about;
But in London, thank heaven! our peace is secure,
Where for one eye to kill, there's a thousand to cure.

I know Love's a devil, too subtle to spy,
That shoots through the soul, from the beam of an eye;
But in London these devils so quick fly about,
That a new devil still drives an old devil out.

In town let me live then, in town let me die;
For in truth I can't relish the country, not I.
If one must have a villa in summer to dwell,
Oh, give me the sweet shady side of Pall Mall!

CAPTAIN CHARLES MORRIS
[1745–1838]

## *Business Girls*

From the geyser ventilators
    Autumn winds are blowing down
On a thousand business women
    Having baths in Camden Town.

Waste pipes chuckle into runnels,
    Steam's escaping here and there,
Morning trains through Camden cutting
    Shake the Crescent and the Square.

Early nip of changeful autumn,
    Dahlias glimpsed through garden doors,
At the back precarious bathrooms
    Jutting out from upper floors.

And behind their frail partitions
    Business women lie and soak.
Seeing through the draughty skylight
    Flying clouds and railway smoke.

Rest you there, poor unbelov'd ones,
    Lap your loneliness in heat.
All too soon the tiny breakfast,
    Trolley-bus and windy street!

SIR JOHN BETJEMAN
[b. 1906]

# THE MOB

*'You know, Ellie has remarkable strength of character. I think it is because I taught her to like Shakespeare when she was very young.'*

Mazzini Dunn to Mrs Hesione Hushabye, in George Bernard Shaw's *Heartbreak House*, 1917.

(A doorkeeper at St James's Palace hears about the crowd that has broken into Palace Yard in order to be present at the christening of King Henry the Eighth's daughter, Elizabeth, the future Queen Elizabeth I.)

## From: *King Henry the Eighth,*
## *Act 5, Scene 3*

|  |  |
|---|---|
| *A voice from without:* | Good master porter, I belong to the larder. |
| Porter | Belong to the gallows, and be hanged, ye rogue! Is this a place to roar in? Fetch me a dozen crab-tree staves, and strong ones: these are but switches to 'em. I'll scratch your heads: you must be seeing christenings? do you look for ale and cakes here, you rude rascals? |
| Man | Pray, sir, be patient: 'tis as much impossible – Unless we sweep 'em from the door with cannons – To scatter 'em, as 'tis to make 'em sleep On May-day mornings. |
| Porter | How got they in, and be hang'd? |
| Man | Alas, I know not; how gets the tide in? As much as one sound cudgel of four foot – You see the poor remainder – could distribute, I made no spare, sir. |
| Porter | You did nothing, sir. |
| Man | I am not Samson, nor Sir Guy, nor Colbrand, To mow 'em down before me: but if I spared any That had a head to hit, either young or old, |

He or she, cuckold or cuckold-maker
Let me ne'er hope to see a chine again
And that I would not for a cow, God save her!

*A voice*
*from without:* Do you hear, master porter?

Porter I shall be with you presently, good master puppy. Keep the door close, sirrah.

Man What would you have me do?

Porter What should you do, but knock 'em down by the dozens? Is this Moorfields to muster in? or have we some strange Indian with the great tool come to court, the women so besiege us? Bless me, what a fry of fornication is at door! On my Christian conscience, this one christening will beget a thousand; here will be father, godfather, and all together.

Man There is a fellow somewhat near the door, he should be a brazier by his face, for, o' my conscience, twenty of the dog-days now reign in 's nose; all that stand about him are under the line, they need no other penance: that fire-drake did I hit three times on the head, and three times was his nose discharged against me; he stands there, like a mortar-piece, to blow us. There was a haberdasher's wife of small wit near him, that railed upon me till her pinked porringer fell off her head, for kindling such a combustion in the state. I missed the meteor once, and hit that woman, who cried out 'Clubs!' when I might see from far some forty truncheoners draw to her succour, which were the hope o' the Strand, where she was quartered. They fell on; I made good my place: at length they came to the broomstaff to me; I defied 'em still: when suddenly a file of boys behind 'em, loose shot, delivered such a shower of pebbles, that I was fain to draw mine honour in and let 'em win the work; the devil was amongst 'em, I think, surely.

Porter These are the youths that thunder at a playhouse and fight for bitten apples; that no audience, but the tribulation of Tower-hill, or the limbs of Limehouse, their dear brothers, are able to endure. I have some of 'em in Limbo Patrum, and there they are like to dance these three days; besides the running banquet of two beadles that is to come.

## WILLIAM SHAKESPEARE
### [1564–1616]

Mentioned: *May-day mornings*, see p. 81; *Samson*, see Judges XVI, 3; *Sir Guy* and *Colbrand*, Sir Guy of Warwick, an early English hero who slew Colbrand the Giant Dane in single combat outside the walls of Winchester, see Ellis, *Specimens of Early English Metrical Romances*, 2, pp. 194, *Moorfields*, a fen to the north of Tudor London, first drained in 1527 and used thereafter for the exercising of trainbands; *strange Indian with the great tool*, an earlier Great Plenipotentiary? – see p. 29; *Limbo Patrum*, prison.

## *Miss Ellen Gee of Kew*

Peerless yet hopeless maid of Q,
Accomplish'd L N G;
Never again shall I and U
Together sip our T.

For oh! the fates, I know not Y,
Sent 'midst the flowers a B;
Which ven'mous stung her in the I,
So that she could not C.

L N exclaimed, 'Vile spiteful B,
　　If ever I catch U
On jessmine, rosebud or sweet P,
　　I'll change your singing Q.

'I'll send you like a lamb or U,
　　Across the Atlantic C;
From our delightful village Q,
　　To distant O Y E.

A stream runs from my wounded I,
　　Salt as the briny C,
As rapid as the X or Y,
　　The O I O or D.

'Then fare thee ill, insensate B,
　　Which stung nor yet knew Y,
Since not for wealthy Durham's C
　　Would I have lost my I.'

They bear with tears poor L N G
　　In funeral R A,
A clay cold corse now doomed to B,
　　Whilst I mourn her D K.

Ye nymphs of Q, then shun each B,
　　List to the reason Y;
For should A B C U at T,
　　He'll surely sting your I.

Now in a grave L deep in Q,
　　She's cold as cold can B;
Whilst robins sing upon A U,
　　Her dirge and L E G.

[c. 1928]

5,000 tons was the weight of a large ship when, in 1858, Queen Victoria stepped aboard Isambard Kingdom Brunel's 18,914 ton *Leviathan* and allowed the anonymous poet to complain about the river's pollution. The *Leviathan* (afterwards the *Great Eastern*) ruined her builder, John Scott Russell, and brought Brunel (1806–1859) to an early grave; nowadays the Thames is much cleaner.

## *Queen Victoria Goes Boating*

What sight was that which loyal eyes
Beheld with horror – not surprise –
    On Thames's filthy tide,
Which bore Victoria, England's Queen
Who, down the River having been,
And the *Leviathan* ship seen,
    Back to her palace hied?

Familiar with the River's smell
Who cannot fancy, all too well,
    The odour which prevailed,
Which rose from the polluted stream
As thick, but not so white, as cream,
And in a suffocating steam,
    The Royal sense assailed?

How shall I state what thousands saw,
Indignant, yet oppressed with awe,
    Their blood which well nigh froze?
The River's perfume was so vile,
The Sovereign, as she neared Dogs' Isle,
Was fain to hold – nay do not smile –
    A bouquet to her nose.

Where shall the Constitution go,
If sewage shall much longer flow,
   The banks, old Thames, between?
The Lords and Commons, by thy breath,
Which both their Houses poisoneth,
Thou sickenest almost to death,
   And hast not spared the Queen!

[1858]

*A View of Westminster from Battersea*

The ceremony for the arrival of the keys, which is performed each night.

> *Sentry:* Halt! Who comes there?
> *Chief Warder:* The Keys.
> *Sentry:* Whose Keys?
> *Chief Warder:* Queen Elizabeth's Keys.
> *Sentry:* Advance Queen Elizabeth's Keys. All's well. (Guard and escort present arms in honour of the Keys).
> *Chief Warder:* (advancing two paces in front of the escort and removing his hat) God preserve Queen Elizabeth.
> *Guard and Escort:* Amen.

*To a City Steeple*

Thou hollow, noisy, proud, aspiring steeple,
   Uttering forth loudly *that* thou dost not feel:
   A mournful now, and now a joyous peal;
Thou dost resemble very many people,
Who even now do act the self-same part,
   Full of condolement and congratulation,
   As doth become the beings of high station,
Much moved in tongue, but little moved in heart:
And on thy top a gilded thing is turning
   Which ever way the wind blows: – strangely strong
Is the resemblance, and to the discerning
   That veering vane doth well befit thy song:
Not to the giddy crowd – *their* upturn'd faces
Will worship any voice that comes from lofty places.

CHARLES LAMB
[1775–1834]

*Boy at Pie Corner*

# The Plague, the Great Fire, St Paul's Cathedral, and Westminster Abbey

Of the 460,000 Londoners at the beginning of 1665, one out of seven was dead of the plague by the time the Great Fire destroyed a fifth of the city in 1666. Some thirty-two longish poems were written about the conflagration, four of them by a Puritan divine called Simon Ford (1619?–1699), who became known as the Laureate of Fire and may well have been the butt of the wit who remarked that the Fire 'created more bad poetry than it destroyed'. Ford glanced at the pest as well as the flames. These, rather good, lines come from his *Conflagration of London Poetically Delineated* (1667):

> Long had the pest with an infectious breath
> From emptied houses throng'd the Gates of Death.
> The Bed-man's tumbrill no distinction made:
> Where once their dirt, chief citizens were lay'd:
> The Sexton oft the grave himself did fill,
> He digg'd for others; oft the Weekly Bill
> Swell'd with its makers; oft it did betide,
> That who lay'd out his friend, lay by his side:
> When (th' barking Star twice lodg'd) 'twas hoped withall
> A second Autumn would not prove a Fall.
> But, trusted hope, like bankrupts, doth compound.
> For ere the long contagious air grew sound,
> And from th' excess of pestilential heat,
> London's pulse did to healthful measure beat,
> A far more doleful fever her befalls.

A fatal fire conceiv'd in private walls,
Nurs'd by contempt, at last grows past arrest;
Defies all aides, and scorns to be supprest.

Three good things came of the Great Fire: the establishment of fire insurance, the building of St Paul's, and the composition of the following lines.

## From: *Annus Mirabilis*

As when some dire usurper Heav'n provides
To scourge his country with a lawless sway:
His birth perhaps some petty village hides,
And sets his cradle out of fortune's way.

Till fully ripe his swelling Fate breaks out,
And hurries him to mighty mischiefs on:
His Prince, surpriz'd at first, no ill could doubt,
And wants the pow'r to meet it when 'tis known.

Such was the rise of his prodigious Fire,
Which in mean buildings first obscurely bred,
From thence did soon to open streets aspire,
And straight to palaces and temples spread.

The diligence of the trades and noiseful gain,
And luxury, more late, asleep were laid:
All was the nights, and in her silent reign
No sound the rest of Nature did invade.

In this deep quiet, from what source unknown,
Those seeds of Fire their fatal birth disclose;
And first, few scatt'ring sparks about were blown,
Big with the flames that to our ruin rose.

Then, in some close-pent room it crept along,
And, smouldring as it went, in silence fed;
Till th' infant Monster, with devouring strong,
Walk'd boldly upright with exalted head.

Now like some rich or mighty murderer,
Too great for prison, which he breaks with gold,
Who fresher for new mischiefs does appear
And dares the world to tax him with the old:

So scapes th' insulting Fire his narrow jail
And makes small out-lets into open air:
There the fierce winds his tender force assail,
And beat him down-ward to his first repair.

The winds, like crafty courtezans, withheld
His flames from burning, but to blow them more:
And every fresh attempt he is repell'd
With faint denials, weaker than before.

And now, no longer letted of his prey,
He leaps up at it with inrag'd desire:
O'relooks the neighbours with a wide survey,
And nods at every house his threatening Fire.

The ghosts of traitors from the Bridge descend,
With bold fanatick spectres to rejoyce:
About the fire into a dance they bend,
And sing their Sabbath notes with feeble voice.

Now streets grow throng'd and busie as by day:
Some run for buckets to the hallow'd quire:
Some cut the pipes, and some the engines play;
And some more bold mount ladders to the fire.

A key of Fire ran all along the shore,
And lighten'd all the river with a blaze:

The waken'd tides began again to roar,
And wond'ring fish in shining waters gaze.

Old Father Thames rais'd up his reverend head,
But fear'd the fate of Simoeis would return:
Deep in his ooze he sought his sedgy bed,
And shrunk his waters back into his urn.

The Fire, mean time walks in a broader gross;
To either hand his wings he opens wide:
He wades the streets, and streight he reaches cross,
And plays his longing flames on th' other side.

At first they warm, then scorch, and then they take;
Now with long necks from side to side they feed:
At length, grown strong, their mother-fire forsake,
And a new colony of flames succeed.

Thus fighting Fires a while themselves consume,
But streight like Turks, forc'd on to win or die,
They first lay tender bridges of their fume,
And o're the breach in unctuous vapours flie.

Part stays for passage, 'till a gust of wind
Ships o're their forces in a shining sheet:
Part, creeping under ground, their journey blind,
And, climbing from below, their fellows meet.

The rich grow suppliant, and the poor grow proud:
Those offer mighty gain, and these ask more;
So void of pity is th' ignoble crowd,
When others ruin may increase their store.

As those who live by shores with joy behold
Some wealthy vessel split or stranded nigh;
And from the rocks leap down for shipwrack'd gold,
And seek the tempest which the others flie:

So these but wait the owners last despair,
And what's permitted to the flames invade:
Ev'n from their jaws they hungry morsels tear,
And, on their backs, the spoils of Vulcan lade.

Those who have homes, when home they do repair,
To a last lodging call their wand'ring friends:
Their short uneasie sleeps are broken with care,
To look how near their own destruction tends.

Those who have none, sit round where once it was,
And with full eyes each wonted room require:
Haunting the yet warm ashes of the place,
As murder'd men walk where they did expire.

Some stir up coals, and watch the vestal fire,
Others in vain from sight of ruin run;
And, while through burning lab'rinths they retire,
With loathing eyes repeat what they would shun.

The most in fields like herded beasts lie down,
To dews obnoxious on the grassy floor;
And while their babes in sleep their sorrows drown,
Sad parents watch the remnants of their store.

Now down the narrow streets it swiftly came,
And, widely opening, did on both sides prey:
This benefit we sadly owe the Flame,
If only ruin must enlarge our way.

And now four days the sun had seen our woes;
Four nights the moon beheld th' incessant fire;
It seem'd as if the stars more sickly rose,
And farther from the feav'rish north retire.

At length th' Almighty cast a pitying eye,
And mercy softly touch'd his melting breast:

He saw the towns one half in rubbish lie,
And eager flames drive on to storm the rest.

As when sharp frosts had long constrain'd the earth,
A kindly thaw unlocks it with mild rain,
And first the tender blade peeps up to birth,
And streight the green fields laugh with promis'd grain:

By such degrees the spreading gladness grew
In every heart, which fear had froze before:
The standing streets with so much joy they view,
That with less grief the perish'd they deplore.

JOHN DRYDEN
[1631–1700]

Old St Paul's was in a bad condition when the Fire helped to destroy it. In 1561 a bolt of lightning knocked its steeple down; in the same year Henry VIII diced its bells away to Sir Miles Partridge. In 1642 Parliament closed it. A few years later it stood a yard deep in horse-dung. Long after Wren rebuilt it, William Woty (1731–1791) preferred Westminster Abbey:

## From *Church Langton*

Gothic the Style, and tending to excite
Free-thinkers to a sense of what is right,
With lengthening aisle, and windows that impart
A gloomy steady light to cheer the heart,
Such as affects the soul, and which I see
With joy, celestial Westminster! in thee.
Not like Saint Paul's, beneath whose ample dome,
No thought arises of the life to come.
For, tho' superb, not solemn is the place,

The mind but wanders o'er the distant space,
Where 'stead of thinking on the God, most men
Forget his presence to remember Wren.

And nowadays:

Sir Christopher Wren
Said, 'I am going to dine with some men.
'If anybody calls
'Say I am designing St Paul's.'

E. C. BENTLEY
[1875–1956]

## Holy Smoke

I am the Vicar of St Paul's
And I'm ringing the steeple bell,
The floor of the church is on fire,
Or the lid has come off hell.

Shall I ring the fire brigade?
Or should I trust in the Lord?
Oh dear! I've just remembered,
I don't think we're insured!

'What's this then?' said the fire chief.
'Is this Church C of E?
It is? Then we can't put it out,
My lads are all RC!'

SPIKE MILLIGAN
[b. 1918]

## *Look at the View*

Like the memory of a long-dead clerical uncle
Reclines St Paul's Cathedral
In the blue smoke from London's frying-pan.
Climb to the dome, and then you can
Watch the dull length of Blackfriar's Bridge.
See the flat girl approach the edge,
Jump, fall, splash, vanish, struggle, cease.
Do you bet she'll be saved by the River Police
Who ride the tides in a humming launch?
Or an oil millionaire without a paunch
Will dive and take her wet to lunch?
Save her and leave her, and she'll be seen
Next day on the bridge near that tarnished tureen
St Paul's Cathedral, glowering in the rain.
She will take off her shoes and fall again.

ADRIAN MITCHELL
[b. 1932]

*View of St Paul's*

More plainly now, as o'er the tide
With swift, but gentle cause we glide;
The sight embraces in its ken
Those dwellings of illustrious men,
Where Thames upon his banks descries
The brave, the courteous and the wise.
But, oh! that sight too well recalls
The name of one, whose love was shrined
Within his river-seated halls.

Yet, while we muse on Time's career,
And hail his care-worn kindred here,
The streaming river bears us on
To London's mighty Babylon:
And that vast Bridge, which proudly soars,
Where Thames through nineteen arches roars,
And many a lofty dome on high
It raises towering to the sky.

There are, whose breth is void of stain,
Who write, in Lion Richard's reign,
That o'er these waves extended stood
A ruder fabric, framed of wood;
But when the swift-consuming flames
Destroyed that bulwark of the Thames,
Rebuilt of stone it rose to view,
Beneath King John its splendours grew,
Whilst London poured her wealth around,
The mighty edifice to found;
The lasting monument to raise
To his, to her eternal praise,
Till, rearing up its form sublime,
It stands the glory of all time.

Yet here we may not longer stay,
But shoot the Bridge and dart away.
Though, with resistless fall, the tide
Is dashing on the bulwark's side
And roaring torrents drown my song,
As o'er the surge I drift along.

## JOHN LELAND
## [1506–1552]

John Leland was one of the first Englishmen to learn Greek. He went mad in 1550.

Taylor was one of 40,000 Thames watermen. For a bet he rowed from London to Queensborough in a paper boat with a pair of flat-fish for oars. Falling out with the poet William Fennor, they agreed to insult each other in verse, in public, and hired Hope's stage, Bankside, for the event. Fennor did not turn up. The audience lost their patience, pelted Taylor with offal, and threw him into the river. Soon afterwards he decided to walk to Scotland. The poem describing his journey begins (and continues) in this way:

> When in the morning I began to go
> Good drinking fellows flocked about me so
> By noon I got no further than the Whale,
> And did full justice to the landlord's ale.
> Thereafter, haste made waste, and sun was set
> Ere to the Shoreditch Flagon I could get.
> At ten I took my leave, and by the moon
> Reached the Bell Inn, and fell into a swoon.
> On Wednesday morning, between eight and nine,
> Well rigged and ballasted with beer and wine
> (For Mrs Croakum of the Rose and Tun
> Knocked on my door before the rising sun)
> I, stumbling forward, thus my jaunt began,
> And by eleven gained the Finsbury Ram.
> There did my childhood friend, the host, begin
> To entertain me freely at his Inn,
> Till all the world had drowned his mortal trunk
> And only No-Body was three parts drunk.
> But in the end I said farewell, and late
> Reached the Blue Boar, that's extra Aldersgate.
> There I did drink, for naught save friendship's sake,
> And travelled full two miles my thirst to break,
> Leaving my host unto his matchless fame,
> And to fair Highgate in the evening came,
> Where Mr Taylor, of the Saracen's Head
> Unasked, unpaid for, helped me into bed.
> At dawn next day I rose, and strode along
> Until at noon I reached the Edgware Swan . . .

John Milton, England's finest poet, was born in Bread Street, Cheap-side. His father was a scrivener. John Aubrey says Milton had dark grey eyes, auburn hair, a delicate, tuneable voice, an exceptional memory, and was slender. At forty-four Milton became blind. At nine p.m. he would drink water, listen to some Ovid, and go to bed. Rising at five he would say: 'I am waiting to be milked'; then he would dictate up to fifty lines of *Paradise Lost* to his daughter, Deborah. It took five years, or thereabouts. He was buried in St Giles, Cripplegate. Many people came. Milton pinned the following sonnet to the door of his house in Aldersgate. It commemorates November 13, 1642, when an army of 24,000 Londoners opposed the Royalist army at Turnham Green. Charles ordered his soldiers to retreat.

## *When the Assault Was Intended to the City*

Captain or colonel, or knight in arms,
　　Whose chance on these defenceless doors may seize,
　　If deed of honour did thee ever please,
　　Guard them, and him within protect from harms,
He can requite thee, for he knows the charms
　　That call fame on such gentle acts as these,
　　And he can spread thy name o'er lands and seas,
　　Whatever clime the sun's bright circle warms.
Lift not thy spear against the muses' bower,
　　The great Emathian conqueror bid spare
　　The house of Pindarus, when temple and tower
Went to the ground: and the repeated air
　　Of sad Electra's poet had the power
　　To save the Athenian walls from ruin bare.

### JOHN MILTON
### [1608–1674]

Mentioned: *Emathian conqueror*, Alexander the Great; *Electra's poet*, the recitation of the first chorus of Euripides' *Electra* is said to have stopped the Thebans sacking Athens in 404 BC.

# Blake's London

Last night in Notting Hill
I saw Blake passing by
who saw Ezekiel
airborne in Peckham Rye.

William Blake, the son of a hosier, was born in what is now called Broadwick Street, W1. He wrote poetry from the age of twelve. Blake taught his wife, Catherine Boucher, to read, write, draw, and paint; with her help he earned his living as a printer and engraver. In 1787 a new method of illuminated printing was revealed to Blake by the spirit of his dead brother, Robert. Blake died while singing.

## London

I wander through each chartered street
Near where the chartered Thames does flow,
And mark in every face I meet
Marks of weakness, marks of woe.

In every cry of every man,
In every infant's cry of fear,
In every voice, in every ban,
The mind-forged manacles I hear –

How the chimney-sweeper's cry
Every blackening church appalls,
And the hapless soldier's sigh
Runs in blood down palace walls;

But most through midnight streets I hear
How the youthful harlot's curse
Blasts the new-born infant's tear
And blights with plagues the marriage hearse.

From: *Songs of Experience*
[1794]

\*

Holy Thursday, the fortieth day after Easter, was marked by a procession of children from the Charity Schools through the city to St Paul's Cathedral. The children were led by their parish Beadles in official dress. Blake's poem comes from his satire, *An Island in the Moon* (c. 1784).

## *Holy Thursday*

'Twas on a holy Thursday, their innocent faces clean,
The children walking two and two, in red, and blue, and green:
Grey-headed beadles walked before, with wands as white as snow,
Till into the high dome of St Paul's they like Thames waters flow.

O what a multitude they seemed, these flowers of London town!
Seated in companies they sit, with radiance all their own.
The hum of multitudes was there, but multitudes of lambs,
Thousands of little boys and girls raising their innocent hands.

Now like a mighty wind they raise to heaven the voice of song,
Or like harmonious thunderings the seats of heaven among:
Beneath them sit the aged men, wise guardians of the poor.
Then cherish pity, lest you drive an angel from your door.

WILLIAM BLAKE
[1757–1827]

# In Bunhill Fields

Bunhill Fields, in Finsbury, is one of London's most famous graveyards. From about 1650 to 1852 it was the favourite burial ground of those who Dissented; John Bunyan, Daniel Defoe, William Blake, and Susanna Wesley, the mother of John and Charles Wesley, among them. In the 1960s certain powerful busybodies had the impudence to move Blake's remains to Westminster Abbey.

> In Bunhill Fields poor Blake's bones lie
> And with the city workers I
> At each pulse of the rush-hour pass
> And pray his sleep beneath the grass
> Remains unpurged of all its dreams;
> For even now the harlot screams.
> England has always had the need
> For those to whom it paid no heed
> And with your pen and prophet's eye
> What horrors of atomic sky
> Could your bright pages so enscribe
> Upon the conscience of the tribe
> That they might act for once as men
> And so prevent what all condemn.

MARTIN GREEN
[b. 1932]

In Paris, in the 1950s, the stir that resulted from the publication of a book of poems by a child called Minou Drouet was squashed by Cocteau's saying: 'All children are poets – except Minou Drouet.'

We four kings of Leicester Square
Selling ladies' underwear:
   How fantastic!
   No elastic!
Only 15p per pair.

\*

Six Jews come from Juda Spain
For your daughter Mary Jane.
Mary Jane is far too young
   To marry you
   You Spanish Jew.
Then farewell, I walk away,
I will come another day.
   Yoo Hoo!
   You Hoo!
Please come back dear Spanish Jew
Choose the fairest of we three.
The fairest one that I can see
Is Dolly Hayes – so come with me.

(Holborn)

\*

I went to the pictures next Tuesday
And took a front seat at the back.
I said to the lady behind me,
I cannot see over your hat.
She gave me some well-broken biscuits,
I ate them and gave her them back;
I fell from the pit to the gallery
And broke my front bone at the back.

(Enfield)

\*

I had a black man, he was double-jointed,
  I kissed him
  I kissed him
I made him disappointed.
Hilda, Hilda, is your scorner,
Kissed a black man round the corner.
How many kisses did he give you?
One, two, three, and three, one, two.

(Notting Hill)

\*

Vote, vote, vote, for Mr Gladstone,
Chuck old Dizzy out the door.
If it wasn't for the law,
I would punch him on the jaw,
We don't want Dandy Dizzy any more!

(Westminster)

\*

As I was walking through the City
Half-past nine o'clock at night
There I met a Spanish lady
Washing out her clothes at night.
First she scrubbed them
Then she rubbed them
Then she hung them up to dry,
Then she laid her hands upon them,
Saying: Come July!

(Bethnal Green)

\*

One, two, three,
Mother caught a flea,
Put it in the tea-pot
And made a cup of tea.
The flea jumped out,
Mother gave a shout,
In came father
With his shirt hanging out.

(Lambeth)

Let others chaunt a country praise,
Fair river walks and meadow ways;
Dearer to me my sounding days
      In London Town:
To me the tumult of the street
Is no less music, than the sweet
Surge of the wind among the wheat,
      By dale or down.

Three names mine heart with rapture hails,
With homage: Ireland, Cornwall, Wales:
Lands of lone moor, and mountain gales,
      And stormy coast:
Yet London's voice upon the air
Pleads at mine heart, and enters there;
Sometimes I wellnigh love and care
      For London most.

Listen upon the ancient hills:
All silence! save the lark, who trills
Through sunlight, save the rippling rills:
      There peace may be.
but listen to great London! loud,
As thunder from the purple cloud,
Comes the deep thunder of the crowd,
      And heartens me.

O gray, O gloomy skies! What then?
Here is a marvellous world of men;
More wonderful than Rome was, when
      The world was Rome!
See the great stream of life flow by!
Here thronging myriads laugh and sigh,
Here rise and fall, here live and die:
      In this vast home.

Gleaming with sunlight, each soft lawn
Lies fragrant beneath dew of dawn;
The spires and towers rise, far withdrawn,
    Through golden mist:
At sunset, linger beside Thames:
See now, what radiant lights and flames!
That ruby burns: that purple shames
    The amethyst.

Winter was long, and dark, and cold:
Chill rains! Grim fogs, black fold on fold,
Round street, and square, and river rolled!
    Ah, let it be:
Winter is gone! Soon comes July,
With wafts from hayfields by-and-by:
While in the dingiest courts you spy
    Flowers fair to see.

Take heart of grace: and let each hour
Break gently into bloom and flower:
Winter and sorrow have no power
    To blight all bloom.
One day, perchance, the sun will see
London's entire felicity:
And all her loyal children be
    Clear of all gloom.

A dream? Dreams often dreamed come true:
Our world would seem a world made new
To those, beneath the churchyard yew
    Laid long ago!
When we beneath like shadows bide,
Fair London, throned upon Thames' side,
May be our children's children's pride:
    And we shall know.

LIONEL JOHNSON
[1867–1902]

# *London*
# *Epitaphs*

'The object of an epitaph is to identify the resting place of the mortal remains of a dead person. It should therefore record only such information as is reasonably necessary for that purpose.'
*The Churchyard Handbook*

Abiding by this rule, the parish register of St Clement Dane's Church records the death of the poet Thomas Otway thus:

1685. Thomas Otway, a man, buried 16 April.

which is bettered by the stone:

THORPE'S
CORPSE
(Hampstead, 1930)

John Dunton's *The Pilgrim's Guide from the Cradle to His Deathbed. To Which Is Added the Sick Man's Passing Bell,* a popular book of 1684, contains this warning about the use of public graveyards:

Dig but a foot or two to make
A cold bed for thy dead friend's sake
'Tis odds but in that tiny room
Thou rob'st some Great Man of his Tomb:
And in thy delving smi'st upon
His shinbone or his cranium.

\*

## HANNA

Stranger, pause,
My tale attend,
And learn the cause
Of Hanna's end.

Across the world
The winds did blow,
She caught a chill,
She lies below.

We shed a quart
Of tears – 'tis true;
But life is short:
Aged 92.

(Hackney, 1944)


Of the next epitaph the composer and instrumentalist Fritz Spiegl says
that Snow was Handel's First Trumpet player; for Snow, Handel
wrote the obbligato 'The Trumpet Shall Sound' in *Messiah*.

Until 1876 the tablet bearing the epitaph could be seen in Wren's All
Hallows Church, Bread Street.

## VALENTINE
## SNOW

Thaw evr'y breast
Melt ev'r'y eye with Woe
Here's dissolution
By the hand of Death!
To dirt, to water turned
The fairest Snow
O the King's Trumpeter
Has lost his Breath

*

SACRED
*to the memory of*
MAJOR JAMES BRUSH
who was killed by the
accidental discharge of
a pistol by his orderly
14th APRIL 1831
*well done*
*good and faithful servant*

(Woolwich Churchyard: demolished)

*

## ON MRS VANBUTCHEL

On the decease of the above lady, Mr Vanbutchel (a celebrated doctor, of Mount Street, Grosvenor Square) contrived, with the assistance of Dr William Hunter [1718–1783], the great anatomist, so to preserve the body as to give it nearly the appearance of life and health, and put it into a glass case. The embalmed remains of Mrs Vanbutchel are now in the Museum of the College of Surgeons, in Lincoln's Inn Fields.

Here unentomb'd, Vanbutchel's consort lies,
To feed her husband's grief, or charm his eyes:
Faintless and pure her body still remains,
And all its former elegance retains:
Long had disease been preying on her charms,
Till slow she shrunk in death's expecting arms;
When Hunter's skill, in spite of nature's laws,
Her beauties rescued from corruption's jaws;
Bade the pale roses of her cheeks revive,
And her shrunk features seem again to live:
– Hunter, who first conceiv'd the happy thought,
And here at length to full perfection brought.
O lucky husband! blest of heaven,
To thee the privilege is given

A much lov'd wife at home to keep,
Caress, touch, talk to, even sleep
Close by her side, when'er you will,
As quiet as if living still.
And, strange to tell, that fairer she,
And sweeter than alive should be;
Fair, plump, and juicy as before,
And full as tractable, or more.
Thrice happy mortal! envied lot,
What a rare treasure hast thou got;
Who to a woman can lay claim,
Whose temper's every day the same.

\*

MRS MARY TANNER

I was deprived of life by a drunken son:
Sweet Lord of Mercy, see that villain hung!

(Bow, 1877)

\*

On Richard Burbage (1567?–1619), Shakespeare's senior business partner and the principal tragedian of the day:

Exit Burbage

(St Leonard's Shoreditch: demolished)

\*

David Garrick (1717–1779) on William Hogarth (1697–1764):

Farewell! great painter of mankind,
Who reached the noblest point of art,
Whose pictur'd morals charm the mind,
And through the eye correct the heart.

If genius fire thee, reader, stay,
If nature move thee, drop a tear,

If neither touch thee, turn away,
For Hogarth's honour'd dust lies here.

(Chiswick Churchyard)

\*

Horace Walpole (1717–1797) on Baron Theodor von Neuhof (1686?–
1756), an adventurer, crowned King Theodore I of Corsica in 1736,
deposed by the Genoese in 1738:

Near this place is interred
Theodore, King of Corsica,
Who died in this parish Dec. 11, 1756,
Immediately after leaving the King's Bench prison,
By the benefit of the Act of Insolvency,
In consequence of which he resigned
His Kingdom of Corsica
For the use of his creditors.
The grave, great teacher, to a level brings
Heroes and beggars, galley slaves and kings,
But Theodore this moral learn'd ere dead,
Fate pour'd its lessons on his living head,
Bestowed a kingdom and denied him bread.

(St Anne's Soho)

*St Pancras Old Church*

Sir John Suckling was a sandy haired card-sharp. He invented the game of cribbage. According to John Aubrey he was sick-livered, red-nosed, easily teased, witty, sharp-tongued, and so compulsive a gambler that his sisters would come to the Piccadilly Bowling Green, crying: 'He will loose our portions!' Which he did.

When the troubles broke out between Charles the First and Parliament, Suckling became involved in a plan to raid the Tower of London. The plan went wrong, Suckling fled to France, and was condemned for high treason *in absentia*. Some say that he was murdered by his servant; others that he died by his own hand.

You will look a long way before finding a better London ballad than:

## *Upon a Wedding*

I tell thee, Dick, where I have been;
Where I the rarest things have seen,
    Oh, things without compare!
Such sights again cannot be found
In any place on English ground,
    Be it at wake or fair.

At Charing Cross, hard by the way
Where we, thou know'st, do sell our hay,
    There is a house with stairs;
And there did I see coming down
Such folk as are not in our town,
    Forty at least, in pairs.

Amongst the rest, one pest'lent fine
(His beard no bigger though than thine)
    Walk'd on before the rest:
Our landlord looks like nothing to him;
The King (God bless him), 'twould undo him,
    Should he go still so dress'd.

At course-a-park, without all doubt,
He should have first been taken out
　　By all the maids i' th' town,
Though lusty Roger there had been,
Or little George upon the green,
　　Or Vincent of the Crown.

But wot you what? the youth was going
To make an end of all his wooing;
　　The Parson for him stay'd:
Yet by his leave, for all his haste,
He did not so much wish all past,
　　Perchance, as did the maid.

The maid – and thereby hangs a tale;
For such a maid no Whitsun-ale
　　Could ever yet produce:
No grape that's kindly ripe could be
So round, so plump, so soft as she,
　　Nor half so full of juice.

Her finger was so small, the ring
Would not stay on which they did bring,
　　It was too wide a peck;
And to say truth (for out it must)
It look'd like the great collar (just)
　　About our young colt's neck.

Her feet beneath her petticoat
Like little mice stole in and out,
　　As if they fear'd the light;
But oh! she dances such a way,
No sun upon an Easter day
　　Is half so fine a sight.

He would have kiss'd her once or twice,
But she would not, she was so nice,

She would not do 't in sight;
And then she look'd as who should say,
I will do what I list to-day,
  And you shall do 't at night.

Her cheeks so rare a white was on,
No daisy makes comparison,
  (Who sees them is undone);
For streaks of red were mingled there,
Such as are on a Katherine pear
  (The side that's next the sun).

Her lips were red, and one was thin
Compar'd to that was next her chin –
  Some bee had stung it newly;
But, Dick, her eyes so guard her face,
I durst no more upon them gaze
  Than on the sun in July.

Her mouth so small, when she does speak,
Thou'dst swear her teeth her words did break,
  That they might passage get;
But she handled still the matter,
They came as good as ours, or better,
  And are not spent a whit.

If wishing should be any sin,
The Parson himself had guilty bin,
  She look'd that day so purely;
And did the youth so oft the feat
At night, as some did in conceit,
  It would have spoil'd him surely.

Just in the nick the cook knock'd thrice,
And all the waiters in a trice
  His summons did obey,
Each serving man with dish in hand,

Marcht boldly up, like our train'd band,
    Presented, and away.

When all the meat was on the table,
What man of knife, or teeth, was able
    To stay to be intreated?
And this the very reason was,
Before the Parson could say grace,
    The company was seated.

The bis'nesse of the kitchen's great,
For it is fit that men should eat;
    Nor was it there deni'd:
Passion o' me! How I run on!
There's that that would be thought upon,
    (I trow) besides the bride.

Now hats fly off, and youths carouse;
Healths first go round, and then the house,
    The bride's came thick and thick;
And when 'twas nam'd another's health,
Perhaps he made it hers by stealth.
    (And who could help it, Dick?)

O' th' sudden up they rise and dance;
Then sit again, and sigh, and glance;
    Then dance again and kiss:
Thus several ways the time did pass,
Whilst ev'ry woman wish'd her place,
    And ev'ry man wish'd his.

By this time all were stol'n aside
To counsel and undress the bride;
    But that he must not know:
But yet 'twas thought he guess'd her mind,
And did not mean to stay behind
    Above an hour or so.

When in he came, Dick, there she lay
Like new-fall'n snow melting away,
    ('Twas time, I trow, to part);
Kisses were now the only stay,
Which soon she gave, as who would say,
    Good boy, with all my heart.

But just as Heav'ns would have, to cross it,
In came the bridesmaids with the posset:
    The bridegroom eat in spite;
For had he left the women to 't,
It would have cost two hours to do 't,
    Which were too much that night.

At length the candle's out, and now
All that they had not done they do:
    What that is, who can tell?
But I believe it was no more
Than thou and I have done before
    With Bridget and with Nell.

SIR JOHN SUCKLING
[1609–1642]

# Composed Upon Westminster Bridge, September 3, 1803

Earth has not anything to show more fair:
Dull would he be of soul who could pass by
A sight so touching in its majesty:
This City now doth, like a garment, wear
The beauty of the morning; silent, bare,
Ships, towers, domes, theatres, and temples lie
Open unto the fields, and to the sky;
All bright and glittering in the smokeless air.
Never did sun more beautifully steep
In his first splendour, valley, rock, or hill;
N'er saw I, never felt, a calm so deep!
The river glideth at his own sweet will:
Dear God! the very houses seem asleep;
And all that mighty heart is lying still!

## WILLIAM WORDSWORTH
[1770–1850]

Wordsworth began this sonnet on the roof of a coach taking him to Dover and finished it on the day named in the title. His sister, Dorothy Wordsworth, says in her *Journal* (31 July 1802):

'We left London on Saturday morning at half past five or six, the 31st of July (I have forgot which). We mounted the Dover Coach at Charing Cross. It was a beautiful morning. The City, St Paul's, with the River and a multitude of little Boats, made a most beautiful sight as we crossed Westminster Bridge. The houses were not overhung by their cloud of smoke, and they were spread out endlessly, yet the sun shone so brightly, with such a pure light, that there was even something like the purity of one of nature's own grand spectacles.'

Winthrop Mackworth Praed, the son of a lawyer, was born in Blooms-
bury. At the age of twenty-two he fought a duel over the date of the
Battle of Bunker Hill. Eight years later he became a Member of
Parliament and stopped writing good verse. He remained a politician
until he died of a liver complaint.

Listing the things he scorned, Wordsworth (in his prissy mood) deline-
ates the things Praed loved: what have I to do, asks Wordsworth, 'with
routs, dinners, morning calls, hurry from door to door, the Westminster
election, with endless things about which nobody cares?'

## From *Good-night to the Season*

Good-night to the Season! 'tis over!
   Gay dwellings no longer are gay;
The courtier, the gambler, the lover,
   Are scatter'd like swallows away:
There's nobody left to invite one,
   Except my good uncle and spouse;
My mistress is bathing at Brighton,
   My patron is sailing at Cowes:
For want of a better employment,
   Till Ponto and Don can get out,
I'll cultivate rural enjoyment,
   And angle immensely for trout.

Good-night to the Season! – the lobbies,
   Their changes, and rumours of change,
Which startled the rustic Sir Bobbies,
   And made all the Bishops look strange:
The breaches, and battles, and blunders,
   Perform'd by the Commons and Peers;
The Marquis's eloquent thunders,
   The Baronet's eloquent ears:

Denouncings of Papists and treasons,
    Of foreign dominion and oats;
Misrepresentations of reasons,
    And misunderstandings of notes.

Good-night to the Season! – the rages
    Led off by the chiefs of the throng,
The Lady Matilda's new pages,
    The Lady Eliza's new song;
Miss Fennel's macaw, which at Boodle's
    Is held to have something to say;
Mrs Splenetic's musical poodles,
    Which bark 'Batti Batti' all day;
The pony Sir Araby sported,
    As hot and as black as a coal,
And the Lion his mother imported,
    In bearskins and grease, from the Pole.

Good-night to the Season! – the splendour
    That beam'd in the Spanish Bazaar;
Where I purchased – my heart was so tender –
    A card-case, – a pasteboard guitar; –
A bottle of perfume, – a girdle, –
    A lithograph'd Riego full-grown,
Whom Bigotry drew on a hurdle
    That artists might draw him on stone, –
A small panorama of Seville, –
    A trap for demolishing flies, –
A caricature of the Devil, –
    And a look from Miss Sheridan's eyes.

Good-night to the Season! – another
    Will come with its trifles and toys,
And hurry away, like its brother,
    In sunshine, and odour, and noise.
Will it come with a rose or a briar?
    Will it come with a blessing or curse?

Will its bonnets be lower or higher?
  Will its morals be better or worse?
Will it find me grown thinner or fatter,
  Or fonder of wrong or of right,
Or married, – or buried? – no matter,
  Good-night to the Season, Good-night!

## WINTHROP MACKWORTH PRAED
## [1802–1839]

Mentioned: *the Season*, May to July in wealthy London; '*Batti Batti*', see *Don Giovanni* Act 1; *Riego*, a revolutionary Spanish colonel, executed 1823; *Miss Sheridan*, one of the playwright's three beautiful grand-daughters.

*In Kensington Gardens*

We'ad a bleed'n' sparrer wot
Lived up a bleed'n' spaht,
One day the bleed'n' rain came dahn
An' washed the bleeder aht.

An' as 'e layed 'arf drahnded
Dahn in the bleed'n' street
'E begged that bleed'n' rainstorm
To bave 'is bleed'n' feet.

But then the bleed'n' sun came aht –
Dried up the bleed'n' rain –
So that bleed'n' little sparrer
'E climbed up 'is spaht again.

But, Oh! – the crewel sparrer'awk,
'E spies 'im in 'is snuggery,
'E sharpens up 'is bleed'n' claws
An' rips 'im aht by thuggery!

The moral of this story
Is plain to everyone –
That them wot's up the bleed'n' spaht
Don't get no bleed'n' fun.

[c. 1930]

# *Changes*

What's not destroyed by time's devouring hand?
Where's Troy, and where's the Maypole in the Strand?

REV. JAMES BRANSTON
[1694–1744]


## *On the Demolition of Charing-Cross*

Built by Edward I in 1290, demolished in 1647 by order of the Long Parliament.

Undone, undone the lawyers are,
   They wander about the town,
Nor can find the way to Westminster,
   Now Charing-Cross is down:
At the end of the Strand they make a stand,
   Swearing they are at a loss,
And chaffing say, that's not the way,
   They must go by Charing-Cross.

The Parliament to vote it down,
   Conceived it very fitting,
For fear it should fall, and kill them all,
   In the house as they were sitting.
They were told, god-wot, it had a plot,
   Which made them so hard-hearted,
To give command, it should not stand,
   But be taken down and carted.

But neither man, woman, nor child,
   Will say, I'm confident,
They ever heard it speak one word

Against the Parliament,
An informer swore, it letters bore,
    Or else it had been freed;
I'll take, in troth, my Bible oath,
    It could neither write, nor read.

The Committee said, that verily
    To Popery it was bent;
For aught I know, it might be so,
    For to church it never went.
What with excise, and such device,
    The kingdom doth begin
To think you'll leave them ne'er a cross,
    Without doors nor within.

Methinks the common-council should
    Of it have taken pity,
'Cause, good old Cross, it always stood
    So firmly to the City.
Since crosses you so much disdain,
    Faith, if I were as you,
For fear the King should rule again,
    I'd pull down Tyburn too.

[c. 1647]

# On the Development of Finch's Grotto

Finch's Grotto was a pleasure garden in Southwark. In June 1771 its proprietors advertised: 'Mr Smith to sing Russell's Triumph in the character of a Midshipman. After which will be displayed a Grand Transparent Painting of Fountains with Serpents jetting water. Over the centre arch is a Medallion of Neptune supported by Tritons; on one wing the God is drawn by Sea-horses; on the other wing is Venus rising from the sea. Through the back Arches is a distant prospect of the Ocean. The whole will be Illuminated in the most elegant manner. Horns and Clarionets will play.' Four years later the grotto was destroyed by fire and a road was built over its remains. A local worthy wrote:

> Here herbs did grow
> and flowers sweet
> but now 'tis called
> Saint George's Street.

## Con-traries

### As Sung by Mr Carwichet at *The Gate*

From Greenwich to Richmond, whatever the site,
  I have strayed like Ulysses in Homer,
And I find that no lawyer can London indict,
  For each street, and each spot's, a misnomer.
Cheapside is, for instance, confoundedly dear;
  In Queen Street, a Queen very rare is;
No fans in Fan Alley, nor ships at New Pier –
  O London is full of con-traries.

Pump Court has no pressure; Well Conduit no spring;
  Field Lane is all houses where Jews are;
No partridge in Partridge Way ever takes wing;
  And horses, not hawks, in the Mews are.
Brick Row is a garden; Knott's Walk is a Bow;
  And Manchester Circus a square is;
Not an orange in Orange's Crescent will grow –
  O London is full of con-traries.

Neither water nor bridge is near Bridgewater Stair;
  Fountain Court – bless the mark! – is quite dry grown;
Thread or needle in Threadneedle Street, I declare
  As unlikely in Rye Place is rye grown.
Cock Heath's horizontal; Duke's Level a hill;
  In Fruithanger Yard not a pear is;
The Gate at St Giles is changed to The Grill –
  O London is full of con-traries.

Spring's Garden is gloomy; Snow's Grotto – a drain;
  At Freshfields the air has turned spotty;
And what quite a joke is, in Bare Bottom Lane
  You'll see neither a bush nor a botty.
In Red Lion Square, stands the Lilywhite Mouse;
  Change Alley, in truth, never varies;
And Quality Court boasts no nobleman's house –
  O London is full of con-traries.

[c. 1800]

*The House of Lords*

# *Suburbs*

What would-be villas, range'd in dapper pride,
Usurp the fields, and choke the highway side!
Where the prig architect, with style in view,
Has dole'd his houses forth, in two by two;
And rear'd a row upon the plan, no doubt,
Of old men's jaws, with every third tooth out.
Or where, still greater lengths, in taste, to go,
He warps his tenements into a bow;
Nails a scant canvass, propt on slight deal sticks,
Nick-name'd veranda, to the first-floor bricks;
Before the whole, in one snug segment drawn,
Claps half a rood of turf he calls a lawn;
Then, chuckling at his lath-and-plaster bubble,
Dubs it the Crescent – and the rents are double.

Here modest ostentation sticks a plate,
Or daubs Egyptian letters, on the gate,
Informing passengers 'tis 'Cowslip Cot',
Or 'Woodbine Lodge', or 'Mr Pummock's Grot'.
To beautify each close-wedge'd neighbour's door,
A stripe of garden aims at length, before;
Three thin, aquatick poplars, parch'd with drought,
(Vying with lines of lamp posts, fix'd without,)
Behind it pine, to decorate the grounds,
And mark with greater elegance their bounds.
Blest neighbourhood! – but three times blest! – thrice three!
When neighbours (as 'twill happen) disagree;
When grievances break forth, and deadly spite,
'Twixt those whom Fate, and bricklayers, would unite.

GEORGE COLMAN, THE YOUNGER
[1762–1836]

## A Nightmare

I dreamed a dream, perhaps a prophecy!
That London over England spread herself;
Swallowed the Green field and the waving plain,
Till all this island grew one hideous town.
And as I gazed in terror rooted, so
The City seemed to take a dreadful life,
To be a monster that desired and felt;
And still did she perceptibly advance,
Blacken and grasp and seize and wither up.
Northward she spread, and did assimilate
Her sister cities of the loom and wheel
That welcomed her with whirring ecstasies;
She made the sky a pall, and as she moved,
Blighted the breathing forests and the woods,
And where the flowers grew, now her pavement lay.
And all the air grew dark, and there was heard,
In place of rippling wave and whispering wind,
Only the hoot of grinding car, the shriek
And fiery belch of engines to the cloud.

STEPHEN PHILLIPS
[1868–1915]


## A Dream

Forget six counties overhung with smoke,
Forget the snorting steam and piston stroke,
Forget the spreading of the hideous town;
Think rather of the pack-horse on the down,
And dream of London, small, and white, and clean,
The clear Thames bordered by its gardens green.

WILLIAM MORRIS
[1834–1896]

Although he was born in Cheapside, poverty obliged Robert Herrick to live in Devon. There, as the vicar of Dean Prior, he taught his favourite pig to drink out of a mug and, once, when the congregation dozed during what he considered to be his witty preaching, flung his sermon at them. Sent packing by the Puritans in 1648, Herrick came gladly back to London. Fourteen years later he returned to, and died in, Devon.

In Herrick's time Londoners went out into the woodlands surrounding their city and brought home the May. John Stow in his *Survey of London* (1598) says: 'Every man, except impediment, would, on May day in the morning, walk into the sweet meadows and green woods, there to rejoice their spirits with the beauty and savour of sweet flowers, and with the harmony of birds, praising God in their kind.' An event commemorated in Herrick's:

## *Corinna's Going a-Maying*

Get up, get up for shame, the blooming morn
Upon her wings presents the god unshorn.
    See how Aurora throws her fair
    Fresh-quilted colours through the air:
    Get up, sweet slug-a-bed, and see
    The dew bespangling herb and tree.
Each flower has wept and bow'd toward the east
Above an hour since: yet you not dress'd;
    Nay! not so much as out of bed?
    When all the birds have matins said
    And sung their thankful hymns, 'tis sin,
    Nay, profanation to keep in,
Whereas a thousand virgins on this day
Spring, sooner than the lark, to fetch in May.

Rise and put on your foliage, and be seen
To come forth, like the spring-time, fresh and green,
    And sweet as Flora. Take no care
    For jewels for your gown or hair:

Fear not; the leaves will strew
Gems in abundance upon you:
Besides, the childhood of the day has kept,
Against you come, some orient pearls unwept;
Come and receive them while the light
Hangs on the dew-locks of the night:
And Titan on the eastern hill
Retires himself, or else stands still
Till you come forth. Wash, dress, be brief in praying:
Few beads are best when once we go a-Maying.

Come, my Corinna, come; and, coming, mark
How each field turns a street, each street a park
Made green and trimm'd with trees: see how
Devotion gives each house a bough
Or branch: each porch, each door ere this
An ark, a tabernacle is,
Made up of white-thorn neatly interwove;
As if here were these cooler shades of love.
Can such delights be in the street
And open fields and we not see't?
Come, we'll abroad; and let's obey
The proclamation made for May:
And sin no more, as we have done, by staying;
But, my Corinna, come, let's go a-Maying.

There's not a budding boy or girl this day
But is got up, and gone to bring in May.
A deal of youth, ere this, is come
Back, and with white-thorn laden home.
Some have despatch'd their cakes and cream
Before that we have left to dream:
And some have wept, and woo'd, and plighted troth,
And chose their priest, ere we can cast off sloth:
Many a green-gown has been given;
Many a kiss, both odd and even:
Many a glance too has been sent

From out the eye, love's firmament;
Many a jest told of the keys betraying
This night, and locks pick'd, yet we're not a-Maying.

Come, let us go while we are in our prime;
And take the harmless folly of the time.
    We shall grow old apace, and die
    Before we know our liberty.
    Our life is short, and our days run
    As fast away as does the sun;
And, as a vapour or a drop of rain,
Once lost, can ne'er be found again,
    So when or you or I are made
    A fable, song, or fleeting shade,
    All love, all liking, all delight
    Lies drowned with us in endless night.
Then while time serves, and we are but decaying,
Come, my Corinna, come, let's go a-Maying.

### ROBERT HERRICK
### [1591–1674]

Mentioned: *beads*, prayers, a rosary; *green-gown*, a roll in the grass.

# *Nursery Rhymes*

### *London Bridge*

(*c.* 1726)

London Bridge is broken down,
  Broken down, broken down,
London Bridge is broken down,
  My fair lady.

Build it up with wood and clay,
  Wood and clay, wood and clay,
Build it up with wood and clay,
  My fair lady.

Wood and clay will wash away,
  Wash away, wash away,
Wood and clay will wash away,
  My fair lady.

Build it up with bricks and mortar,
  Bricks and mortar, bricks and mortar,
Build it up with bricks and mortar,
  My fair lady.

Bricks and mortar will not stay,
  Will not stay, will not stay,
Bricks and mortar will not stay,
  My fair lady.

Build it up with iron and steel,
  Iron and steel, iron and steel,
Build it up with iron and steel,
  My fair lady.

Iron and steel will bend and bow,
  Bend and bow, bend and bow,
Iron and steel will bend and bow,
  My fair lady.

Build it up with silver and gold,
  Silver and gold, silver and gold,
Build it up with silver and gold,
  My fair lady.

Silver and gold will be stolen away,
  Stolen away, stolen away,
Silver and gold will be stolen away,
  My fair lady.

Set a man to watch all night,
  Watch all night, watch all night,
Set a man to watch all night,
  My fair lady.

Suppose the man should fall asleep,
  Fall asleep, fall asleep,
Suppose the man should fall asleep?
  My fair lady.

Give him a pipe to smoke all night,
  Smoke all night, smoke all night,
Give him a pipe to smoke all night,
  My fair lady.

## Pussy Cat, Pussy Cat

From *Songs for the Nursery*
(1805)

Pussy cat, pussy cat, where have you been?
I've been to London to look at the queen.
Pussy cat, pussy cat, what did you there?
I frightened a little mouse under her chair.

## Oranges and Lemons

from *Tommy Thumb's Pretty Song Book*
(1774)

Oranges and lemons,
Say the bells of St Clement's.

You owe me five farthings,
Say the bells of St Martin's.

When will you pay me?
Say the bells of Old Bailey.

When I grow rich,
Say the bells of Shoreditch.

When will that be?
Say the bells of Stepney.

I'm sure I don't know,
Says the great bell at Bow.

Here comes a candle to light you to bed,
Here comes a chopper to chop off your head.
Chop! Chop! Chop!

## *Bishopsgate*

Bishopsgate Without!
Bishopsgate Within!
What a clamour at the Gate,
O what a din!
Inside and Outside
The Bishops bang and shout,
Outside crying, 'Let me In!'
Inside, 'Let me Out!'

ELEANOR FARJEON
[1881–1965]

*Old London Bridge*

In 1874 Robert Bridges became a doctor; in 1877 he saw 30,940 patients
and prescribed 200,000 doses of medicine containing iron; in 1882 he
stopped doctoring and spent the remainder of his life in rural seclusion.
To the surprise of those who thought that Kipling should get the job, Mr
Asquith made Bridges Poet Laureate in 1913. On his eightieth birthday,
Bridges' admirers gave him a clavichord.

When men were all asleep the snow came flying,
In large white flakes falling on the city brown,
Stealthily and perpetually settling and loosely lying,
    Hushing the latest traffic of the drowsy town;
Deadening, muffling, stifling its murmurs failing;
Lazily and incessantly floating down and down:
    Silently sifting and veiling road, roof and railing;
Hiding difference, making unevenness even,
Into angles and crevices softly drifting and sailing.
    All night it fell, and when full inches seven
It lay in the depth of its uncompacted lightness,
The clouds blew off from a high and frosty heaven;
    And all woke earlier for the unaccustomed brightness
Of the winter dawning, the strange unheavenly glare:
The eye marvelled – marvelled at the dazzling whiteness;
    The ear hearkened to the stillness of the solemn air;
No sound of wheel rumbling nor of foot falling,
And the busy morning cries came thin and spare.
    Then boys I heard, as they went to school, calling,
They gathered up the crystal manna to freeze
Their tongues with tasting, their hands with snowballing;
Or rioted in a drift, plunging up to the knees;
Or peering up from under the white-mossed wonder,
'O look at the trees!' they cried, 'O look at the trees!'
    With lessened load a few carts creak and blunder,
Following along the white deserted way,
A country company long dispersed asunder:
    When now already the sun, in pale display
Standing by Paul's high dome, spread forth below

His sparkling beams, and awoke the stir of the day.
    For now doors open, and war is waged with the snow;
And trains of sombre men, past tale of number,
Tread long brown paths, as toward their toil they go:
    But even for them awhile no cares encumber
Their minds diverted; the daily word is unspoken,
The daily thoughts of labour and sorrow slumber
At the sight of the beauty that greets them, for the charm they have
    broken.

ROBERT BRIDGES
[1844–1930]

# Districts and Places

## Highgate Hill

As I came down the Highgate Hill,
The Highgate Hill, the Highgate Hill,
As I came down the Highgate Hill,
I met the sun's bravado,
And saw below me, fold on fold,
Grey to pearl and pearl to gold,
London like a land of old,
The land of eldorado.

SIR HENRY BASHFORD
[1880–1961]

## Islington

At Islington
　A fair they hold,
Where cakes and ale
　Are to be sold.
At Highgate, and
　At Holloway
The like is kept
　Here every day,
At Totnam Court
　And Kentish Town,
And all those places
　Up and down.

[c. 1676]

## City Road

Up and down the City Road,
   In and out the Eagle,
That's the way the money goes,
   Pop goes the weasel!

Half a pound of twopenny rice,
   Half a pound of treacle,
Mix it up and make it nice,
   Pop goes the weasel!

W. R. MANDALE
[fl· 1890]

*John Wesley's Chapel in the City Road*

# West Smithfield and Bartholomew Fair

Named after St Bartholomew the Apostle, and opening on his day (August 24th) each year from 1133 to 1855, this Fair was the national market for the exchange and sale of cloth. In 1641 it covered four parishes, lasted for fourteen days, and was opened by the Lord Mayor, before whom the Merchant Taylors' Guild paraded their Silver Yard – the measure against which cloth was sold throughout the realm.

## *Bartholomew Fair*

While gentlefolk strut in their silver and satins,
    We others go tramping in bonnets and pattens
And merrily old English ballads will sing-o
    As they will in operays outlandish lingo
Sing bravo, sing caro, encoro, whate'ero,
    But nothing I sing save Bartholomew Fair-o.

Crowd upon crowd upon other crowds driving,
    Shout over shout and each contrary striving,
With fiddling, and fluting, and roaring, and shrieking,
    Drum, fife and trumpet, and barrowgirls squeaking;
My rare round and found take your choice of fine wear-o,
    Tho' sold means not sound at Bartholomew Fair-o.

See the Lady in Leaves, and the Spaniard in Lights,
    The Grandees of France, and the Pig that Recites,
A Cave with a Mermaid, a Cloud with a Dragon,
    And the Duke who can drink his own weight from a flagon;
My rare round and found take your choice of fine wear-o,
    Tho' sold means not sound at Bartholomew Fair-o.

Here are dolls, here are dances, the showing of postures,
    Plum-porridge, black-puddings, and Colchester oysters,
Here is Punch's own play, and the Gunpowder Squire,
    Fine sausages fried, and the Black on the wire;
My rare round and found take your choice of fine wear-o,
    Tho' sold means not sound at Bartholomew Fair-o.

[c. 1750]


## The Cock Tavern, Fleet Street

O plump head-waiter at The Cock,
    To which I most resort,
How goes the time? 'Tis five o'clock,
    Go fetch a pint of port.

LORD TENNYSON
[1809–1892]

## *Bloomsbury*

For me, for me, these old retreats
Amid the world of London streets!
My eye is pleased with all it meets
                    In Bloomsbury

I know how green is Peckham Rye,
And Syd'nham, flashing in the sky,
But did I dwell there I should sigh
                    For Bloomsbury.

I know where Maida Vale receives
The night dews on her summer leaves,
Not less my settled spirit cleaves
                    To Bloomsbury.

Some love the Chelsea river gales,
And the slow barges' ruddy sales,
And these I'll woe when glamour fails
                    In Bloomsbury.

[c. 1893]

# *Soho*

Visitors to London come year after year.
The colour of their skins and their accents may seem queer.
But the spot they all want to see and know,
You've guessed it first time, it's dear old Soho.

Four circuses were built long, long ago –
Piccadilly, Oxford, Cambridge, St Giles – and so
The powers that be in their wisdom so clever
Said: We'll give it a name that lasts for ever and ever.

In those far off days around here they used to hunt,
Horses and hounds were all to the front.
But the cry of the Hunt sounded like 'Ho Ho',
So that's how this place came to be called 'So Ho'.

The first to arrive from the continent were the French
With their habits and costumes and thirsts to quench.
They built their bistros and patisseries and did so well
That the Germans heard about it and came quick as hell.

Italians, Poles, Czechs, Hungarians were the next to arrive.
In a land as good as this they were all bound to survive.
Survive they all did and brought their relations as well,
But this is another story and would take years to tell.

Myself I've lived around here for forty years and more.
Of characters I've met some living, some dead, some rich and some
    poor.
French Letter Syd, Overcoat Charlie, Ironfoot Jack and others.
I've even met some villains who had sisters and brothers.

The Chinese then arrived with their manners so good.
Parts of Gerrard Street suited them, as I knew it would.
Fortunes were made there selling succulent dishes to eat,
And as a result they've taken over the whole bloody street.

FRANCIS BLAKE
[b. 1906]

## The Swedish Giant at Charing Cross

'That Prodigy in Nature the living Colossus or wonderful Giant, from Sweden, now to be seen at the Lottery House next Door to the Green Man, Charing Cross. It is humbly presum'd, that of all the natural Curiosities which have been expos'd to the Publick, nothing has appear'd for many Ages so extraordinary in its Way as this surprising Gentleman. He is much taller than any Person ever yet shewn in Europe, large in Proportion; and all who have hitherto seen him declare, notwithstanding the prodigious Accounts they have heard, that he far exceeds any Idea they had framed of him.

Note, He is to be seen as above any Hour of the Day by any Number of Gentlemen and Ladies, from Nine in the Morning till Nine at Night.'

> Amazing Man! of such stupendous Size,
> As moves, at once, our Wonder and Surprize.
> The Son of Kish (Being Head and Shoulders taller)
> Was chose a King, to govern all the smaller:
> Had you been there, the stately Monarch Saul
> Had had no title to that sacred Call.
> Repair to Oxford, that sublime Retreat,
> The Source of Wisdom and the Muses' Seat;
> Her learned Sons (who rummage Nature's ways)
> Shall come with Pleasure, and with Wonder gaze:
> In every Science there each curious Spark,
> May mark how Nature has o'ershot her Mark.

[1742]

# Rotten Row

There's a tempting bit of greenery – of *rus in urbe* scenery –
  That's haunted by the London 'upper ten';
Where, by exercise on horseback, an equestrian may force back
  Little fits of *tedium vitae* now and then.

Oh! the times that I have been there, and the types that I have seen there
  Of that gorgeous Cockney animal, the 'swell';
And the scores of pretty riders (both patricians and outsiders)
  Are considerably more than I can tell.

When first the warmer weather brought these people all together,
  And the crowds began to thicken through the Row,
I reclined against the railing on a sunny day, inhaling
  All the spirits that the breezes could bestow.

And the riders and the walkers and the thinkers and the talkers
  Left me lonely in the thickest of the throng,
Not a touch upon my shoulder – not a nod from one beholder –
  As the stream of Art and Nature went along.

But I brought away one image, from that fashionable scrimmage,
  Of a figure and a face – ah, *such* a face!
Love has photograph'd the features of that loveliest of creatures
  On my memory, as Love alone can trace.

Did I hate the little dandy in the whiskers, (they were sandy,)
  Whose absurd salute was honour'd by a smile?
Did I marvel at his rudeness in presuming on her goodness,
  When she evidently loathed him all the while?

Oh the hours that I have wasted, the regrets that I have tasted,
  Since the day (it seems a century ago)
When my heart was won *instanter* by a lady in a canter,
  On a certain sunny day in Rotten Row!

HENRY SAMBROKE LEIGH
[1837–1883]

## *A Crow in Bayswater*

A carrion crow flew over Bayswater –
Dews of morning distilled on his dark wings.

Shadows of night retired – the ghost
Of Peter Rachman, pursued
By phantom Alsatian dogs,
Scurried down St Stephen's Gardens.

He sailed over All Saints Church, and Father Clark
Unlocking the door for Anglican Eucharist;

Over spilling dustbins, where
Warfarin-resistant mice
Licked the insides of empty soup-cans,
Worried
Potato peelings, stale sliced bread.

'Cark!' said the crow, a raucous croak – to me
The stern music of freedom –

'I will go to Kensington Gardens;
Down by the Round Pond.
New-hatched ducklings are out:
We'll scrag a couple for breakfast.'

JOHN HEATH-STUBBS
[b. 1918]

## *Notting Hill Polka*

We've – had –
A Body in the house
  Since Father passed away:
He took bad on
Saturday night an' he
  Went the followin' day:

Mum's – pulled –
The blinds all down
  An' bought some Sherry Wine,
An' we've put the tin
What the Arsenic's in
  At the bottom of the Ser-pen-tine!

### W. BRIDGES-ADAMS
### [1889–1965]

## Chelsea Buns

O flour of the ovens! a zephyr in paste!
Fragrant as honey and sweeter in taste!
Hail to the bellman, who sings as he runs,
'Smoking hot, piping hot, Chelsea buns!'

As flaky and white as if baked by the light,
As the flesh of an infant, soft, doughy, and slight;
The public devour thee like Goths and Huns,
'Smoking hot, piping hot, Chelsea buns!'

Prelates, and princes, and lieges, and kings,
Hail for the bellman, who tinkles and sings,
Bouche of the highest and lowliest ones,
'Smoking hot, piping hot, Chelsea buns!'

Like the home of your birth, or the scent of a flower,
Or the blush of the morning on field or bower,
There's a charm in the sound which nobody shuns,
Of 'Smoking hot, piping hot, Chelsea buns!'

[c. 1844]

## Crocus-Time at Hampton Court

To Hampton Court each spring I make
   A pilgrimage on willing feet,
A pilgrimage for beauty's sake
   With scrip and wallet all complete;
With scrip to write each lovely thought
   A poet has whene'er he sees
The crocuses at Hampton Court
   About the grass beneath the trees.

Like gold and purple helmets worn
   By hidden knights who watch me pass,
Like coloured shields by fairies borne
   Among the swordblades of the grass.
A scrip to catch in glowing words
   The beauties that I ponder there;
A wallet full of bread for birds –
   The great, shy birds who wander there.

Each year my scrip remains a blank,
   And vain the poet's pencil is
To paint that lush and lovely bank
   Enamelled by those crocuses,
They will not come for any words,
   For any praise I proffer them –
But, thank the Lord, at least the birds
   Will eat the bread I offer them!

J. H. G. FREEMAN
[b. 1903]

# *Kew*

Go down to Kew in lilac-time, in lilac-time, in lilac-time.
   Go down to Kew in lilac-time (it isn't far from London!),
And you shall wander hand in hand with love in summer's wonderland
   Go down to Kew in lilac-time (it isn't far from London!).

The cherry-trees are seas of bloom and soft perfume and sweet perfume
   The cherry-trees are seas of bloom (and oh, so near to London!),
And there they say when dawn is high and all the world's a blaze of sky
   The cuckoo, though he's very shy, will sing a song for London.

The Dorian nightingale is rare, and yet they say you'll hear him there
   At Kew, at Kew in lilac-time (and oh, so near to London!),
The linnet and the throstle, too, and after dark the long halloo
   And golden-eyed *tu-whit, tu-whoo*, of owls that ogle London.

For Noah hardly knew a bird of any kind that isn't heard
   At Kew, at Kew in lilac-time (and oh, so near to London!),
And when the rose begins to pout and all the chestnut spires are out
   You'll hear the rest without a doubt, all chorussing for London:

*Come down to Kew in lilac-time, in lilac-time, in lilac-time;*
   *Come down to Kew in lilac-time (it isn't far from London!),*
*And you shall wander hand in hand with love in summer's wonderland*
   *Come down to Kew in lilac-time (it isn't far from London!).*

ALFRED NOYES
[1880–1958]

## TWICKENHAM AND RICHMOND

In 1718, with the £9,000 he had earned from his translation of Homer, Alexander Pope (1688–1744), England's most elegant poet to date, bought and moved into a Thames-side house at Twickenham. There, over the next twenty years, he and John Searle, his gardener, designed and planted a garden whose originality and beauty became famous. Visitors entered the garden via a grotto:

> . . . where Thames' translucent wave
> Shines a broad mirror through the shadowy cave;
> Where lingering drops from mineral roofs distil,
> And pointed crystals break the sparkling rill,
> Unpolish'd gems no ray on pride bestow,
> And latent metals innocently glow:
> Approach. Great Nature studiously behold!
> And eye the mine without the wish for gold.

Writing to her sister, the Countess of Mar, Lady Mary Wortley Montagu – *Wortley* in the poem that follows – said: 'I see. . . very seldom Mr Pope, who continues to embellish his house at Twickenham. . . I send you here some verses addressed to Mr Gay, who wrote him a congratulatory letter on the finishing of his house.' Soon after this letter was written Pope and Lady Mary began a lifelong quarrel.

## *To Mr Gay*

> Ah friend, 'tis true – this truth you lovers know –
> In vain my structures rise, my gardens grow,
> In vain fair Thames reflects the double scenes
> Of hanging mountains, and of sloping greens:
> Joy lives not here; to happier seats it flies,
> And only dwells where Wortley casts her eyes.

What are the gay parterre, the chequer'd shade,
The morning bower, the ev'ning colonade,
But soft recesses of uneasy minds,
To sigh unheard in, to the passing winds?

So the struck deer in some sequester'd part
Lies down to die, the arrow at his heart;
There, stretch'd unseen in coverts hid from day,
Bleeds drop by drop, and pants his life away.

## Remembrance of Collins
## Composed upon the Thames near Richmond

William Collins (1721–1759) was the son of a hatter. Disappointed by the public's indifference to his poems he became a melancholy drunkard and died insane. As Pope says:

All this may be; the people's voice is odd,
It is, and it is not, the voice of God.


Glide gently, thus for ever glide,
O Thames! That other bards may see
As lovely visions by thy side
As now, fair river! come to me.
O glide, fair stream! for ever so,
Thy quiet soul on all bestowing,
Till all our minds for ever flow
As thy deep waters now are flowing.

Vain thought! – Yet be as now thou art,
That in thy waters may be seen
The image of a poet's heart,
How bright, how solemn, how serene!
Such as did once the Poet bless,
Who murmuring here a later ditty,
Could find no refuge from distress
But in the milder grief of pity.

Now let us, as we float along,
For *him* suspend the dashing oar;
And pray that never child of song
May know that Poet's sorrows more.
How calm! how still! the only sound,
The dripping of the oar suspended!
– The evening darkness gathers round
By virtue's holiest Powers attended.

WILLIAM WORDSWORTH
[1770–1850]

Last night in London Airport
I saw a wooden bin
labelled UNWANTED LITERATURE
IS TO BE PLACED HEREIN.
So I wrote a poem
and popped it in.

CHRISTOPHER LOGUE
[b. 1926]

*View from Richmond Hill*

It is my pleasure to thank the following Librarians for the patience and the kindness they have shown to me while I was compiling this book: the Staff of the Reading Room, Department of Printed Books, the British Library; the Staff of the Guildhall Library, the City of London; Mr Douglas Matthews and the Staff of the London Library; the Staff of the Reference Library, the Royal Borough of Kensington and Chelsea; Mr Jonathan Barker and the Staff of the Arts Council Poetry Library. May I also thank: Mr Richard Adams of the Open Head Press, Mr Ian Burton, Mr Michael Diamond, Mr Timothy Egan, Mr Albert Garrett, Mr Charles Grahame, Mr Peter Grose, Miss Mary Hurworth, Mr Ralph Hyde, Mr John Marquand, Mr John Michell, Miss Maggie Noach, Miss Helen Owen, Mr Robin Pearson, Mrs Pamela Sladek, Mr Bernard Stone, Ms Emma Tennant and Mr Peter Ward.

Cover      'London, the glory of Great Britain's isle', from a print by Wenceslaus Hollar prefixed to Howell's *Londinopolis*, 1620.

Half-title      *The Home Book of Quotations*, N.Y., 1967.

Page iii      Eric Maschwitz: Extract from 'A Nightingale Sang in Berkeley Square' from *New Faces Revue*, 1940, © Peter Maurice Music Co. Ltd., reprinted by permission of EMI Music Publishing Ltd.

Page vi      Samuel Johnson: (i) Extract from *London*, 1738; (ii) from *Boswell's Life of Johnson: 1777*, ed. Edmund Malone, 1799.

Page 9      William Dunbar: 'To the City of London' from *Scottish Poetry from Barbour to James VI*, ed. M. M. Gray, 1935.

Page 12      George Turberville: 'The Lover to the Thames of London. . .' from *Epitaphs, Epigrams, Songs and Sonnets*, 1567.

Page 13      Lord Byron: from Cantos 10, 11, and 13 of *Don Juan*, ed. T. G. Steffan, E. Steffan and W. W. Pratt, 1973.

Page 20      W. E. Henley: 'Life-Guardsman' from *Poems*, 1921.

Page 21      Candida Lycett-Green: 'Miss Knightsbridge', 1967, reprinted by permission of the author.

Page 22      Evan Jones: 'The Lament of the Banana Man' from *Commonwealth Poems of Today*, ed. Howard Sergeant, 1967.

108

Page 26    Fleur Adcock: 'Miss Hamilton in London' from *Tigers*, 1967, reprinted by permission of Oxford University Press.
Page 28    Thomas Hardy: 'The Ruined Maid' from *Poems of the Past and the Present*, 1901.
Page 29    Capt. Charles Morris: 'The Town and the Country' from *Lyra Urbanica*, 1840.
Page 32    Sir John Betjeman: 'Business Girls' from *Collected Poems*, 1958, reprinted by permission of the author and John Murray Ltd.
Page 33    William Shakespeare: Extract from *King Henry VIII*, written 1612, performed 1613, published 1623.
Page 35    'Miss Ellen Gee of Kew' from *A New Book of Sense and Nonsense*, ed. Ernest Rhys, 1928.
Page 37    'Queen Victoria Goes Boating' from *Punch*, 10th June 1858.
Page 40    Charles Lamb: 'To a City Steeple' from *Works*, ed. E. V. Lucas, 1905.
Page 41    Simon Ford: Extract from 'The Conflagration of London Poetically Delineated', 1667, from Robert Arnold Aubin's *London in Flames, London in Glory*, 1943.
Page 42    John Dryden: Extract from 'Annus Mirabilis' from *The Poetical Works of John Dryden*, ed. The Rev. George Gilfillan, 1885.
Page 46    William Woty: 'Church Langton' from *Poems on Several Occasions*, 1780.
Page 47    E. C. Bentley: 'Sir Christopher Wren' from *The Complete Clerihews of E. Clerihew Bentley* (1981), reprinted by permission of Oxford University Press.
Page 47    Spike Milligan: 'Holy Smoke' from *A Book of Bits*, 1967, Star Books, reprinted by permission of the author.
Page 48    Adrian Mitchell: 'Look at the View' from *For Beauty Douglas*, 1982, reprinted by permission of the author.
Page 49    John Leland: 'Henry VIII and the Thames at London Bridge' (trans. by Richard Thomson) from *Cygnia Cantio*, 1545.
Page 52    John Milton: 'When the Assault Was Intended to the City'

from *The Poems of John Milton*, ed. John Carey and Alastair Fowler, 1968.

Page 53 William Blake: 'London' and 'Holy Thursday' from *Poems*, ed. W. H. Stevenson, 1971.

Page 55 Martin Green: 'In Bunhill Fields' from *Nimbus* Magazine, February 1958, reprinted by permission of the author.

Page 58 Lionel Johnson: Extract from 'London Town' from *Works*, 1915.

Page 60 John Dunton: 'London Epitaphs'; see reference to Simon Ford q.v.

Page 65 Sir John Suckling: 'Upon a Wedding' from *Fragmenta Aurea*, 1646.

Page 70 Dorothy Wordsworth: Extract from her *Journal*, ed. Ernest de Sélincourt, 1941.

Page 70 William Wordsworth: 'Composed Upon Westminster Bridge' from *Poems*, ed. John D. Hayden, 1977.

Page 71 William Wordsworth: Extract, from *The Letters of William and Dorothy Wordsworth*, ed. Ernest de Sélincourt, 1969.

Page 71 Winthrop Mackworth Praed: 'Good-night to the Season' from *Selected Poems of Winthrop Mackworth Praed*, ed. Kenneth Allot, 1953.

Page 75 'On the Demolition of Charing-Cross' from *Reliques of Ancient English Poetry*, ed. Thomas Percy, Bishop of Dromore, 1765.

Page 77 'Con-traries, As sung by Mr Carwichet at *The Gate*', adapted from an anonymous squib in Edward Wedlake Brayley's *Londiniana or Reminiscences of the British Metropolis*, 1828.

Page 79 George Colman, the Younger: 'Suburbs' from '*London Rurality*', *Poetical Vagaries*, 1814.

Page 80 Stephen Phillips: 'A Nightmare' from *Poems*, 1907.

Page 80 William Morris: 'A Dream' from *The Earthly Paradise*, 1868.

Page 81 Robert Herrick: 'Corinna's Going a-Maying' from *The Works of Robert Herrick*, ed. Alfred Pollard, 1898.

Page 87 Eleanor Farjeon: 'Bishopsgate' from *Nursery Rhymes in London*, 1916, reprinted by permission of Gerald Duckworth & Co. Ltd.

Page 88    Robert Bridges: 'London Snow' from *Works*, 1913.

Page 90    Sir Henry Bashford: 'Highgate Hill' from *Songs out of School*, 1916, reprinted by permission of the Estate of the late Sir Henry Bashford.

Page 90    'At Islington' from *Poor Robin's Almanac*, 1676.

Page 92    'Bartholomew Fair', adapted from a poem of that name in *Songs Comic and Satirical*, George Stevens, 1796.

Page 93    Lord Tennyson: 'The Cock Tavern, Fleet Street' from 'Will Waterproof's Lyrical Monologue', *The Poems of Tennyson*, ed. Christopher Ricks, 1969.

Page 95    Francis Blake: 'Soho' from *Tuba* Magazine, No. 14, June 1982, reprinted by permission of the author.

Page 96    'The Swedish Giant at Charing Cross' from the *Daily Advertiser*, 24th April, 1742.

Page 97    Henry Sambroke Leigh: 'Rotten Row' from *Carols of Cockayne*, 1868.

Page 98    John Heath-Stubbs: 'A Crow in Bayswater' from *The Watchman's Flute*, 1978, reprinted by permission of David Higham Associates Ltd.

Page 99    'Painless Dentistry' from *Christmas Tips by the Special Correspondents of the Kensington News* (c. 1875).

Page 99    W. Bridges-Adams: 'Notting Hill Polka' from *To Charlotte While Shaving*, reprinted by permission of A. D. Peters & Co. Ltd.

Page 100    'Chelsea Buns' from *The Penny Magazine*, 1844.

Page 101    J. H. G. Freeman: 'Crocus-Time at Hampton Court' from *Middlesex in Prose and Verse*, ed. T. Michael Pope, 1930.

Page 102    Alfred Noyes: 'Kew' '*The Barrel-Organ*' from *Collected Poems* 1963, reprinted by permission of John Murray Ltd.

Page 103    Alexander Pope: Extract from 'On His Grotto' and 'To Mr Gay' from *Works*, ed. Norman Ault and John Butt, 1954.

Page 104    William Wordsworth: 'Remembrance of Collins Composed upon the Thames near Richmond, from *Poems*, ed. John D. Hayden, 1977.

Page 106 Christopher Logue: 'London Airport' from *Ode to the Dodo, Poems 1953–78*, reprinted by permission of Jonathan Cape Ltd.

Every effort has been made to discover the owners of copyright material reprinted. On receiving notification, any omissions that have occurred will be rectified.

## ILLUSTRATIONS

# BOOKS CONSULTED

John Aubrey: *Brief Lives*, ed. Oliver Lawson Dick, 1949

William Camden: *Remains, with Additions by Philpot*, 1659

*The Churchyards Handbook*, Council for the Care of Churches, 1947

*Cobleriana*, 1768

John Diprose: *Diprose's Book of Epitaphs*, 1879

Norman Douglas: *London Street Games*, 1916

Miles Hadfield: *A History of British Gardening*, 1969

R. J. Ham: *Otway and Lee*, 1931

Charles Hindley: *The Works of John Taylor*, 1872

John Irwin and Jocelyn Herbert: *Sweete Themmes*, 1951

Esmor Jones: *Paved With Gold*, 1975

Hugh and Pauline Massingham: *The London Anthology*, 1950

Helen and Lewis Melville: *London's Lure*, 1909

John D. Mortimer: *An Anthology of the Home Counties*, 1947

Edward Nares: *Heraldic Anomalies*, 1823

Horatio Edward Norfolk: *Gleanings in Graveyards*, 1866

Iona and Peter Opie: *The Lore and Language of Schoolchildren*, 1959
                    *The Oxford Dictionary of Nursery Rhymes*, 1952

Walter S. Scott: *Pride of London*, 1947

Fritz Spiegl: *A Small Book of Grave Humour*, 1971

Wilfred Whitten: *London in Song*, 1898

Robert Wilkinson: *Londina Illustrated*, 1819